The Incredible You

Unleash
Passion, Abundance, Confidence & Expectation

In Your Life

Darnyelle A. Jervey

© *The Incredible You* 2009 by Darnyelle A. Jervey.
All rights reserved. No part of this book may be reproduced, stored in a retrieval system or transmitted in any form by any means without the prior written permission of the publishers, except by a reviewer who may quote brief passages in a review to be printed in a newspaper or journal.

All definitions are from Webster's New World Dictionary Third College Edition © by Prentice Hall.

All scripture references are from The Holy Bible, New International Version copyright ©1984 by International Bible Society and the Zondervan Corporation.

Author photo by Tonja Jennings
Book Cover design by IOE Publications
Edited by Shawndra C. Johnson

ISBN 13: 978-0-9820280-1-8
ISBN 10: 0-9820280-1-6
Library of Congress Control Number: 2008943900

Published by IOE Publications, LLC
www.incredibleoneenterprises.com
560 Peoples Plaza # 255
Newark, Delaware 19702
1-888-801-5794

Printed in the United States of America

Acknowledgements

To God be the Glory for the great things that He has done! God as always, You deserve all that I have because You gave it to me! When I started Incredible One Enterprises, I did it in obedience and accordance to the dream You placed in my heart long ago. Through Your grace and my life experiences, I am finally able to birth my purpose and it is alive and well in Incredible One. Thank you. Even as I type this acknowledgment, I honor Your goodness, Your provision, Your protection and Your priesthood. You are my everything and I thank you. Use me for Your glory, Lord. Equip me to empower the lives of others that they may know their Incredibleness because of the You that resides in each of them.

To Regina Jervey-Evans and Roosevelt Evans, whom I affectionately call "Cookie Monster:" I love you both so much and I am so grateful to have you in my Incredible corner. I am so elated that you are building me up. Mommy, you are so important to me and I am so happy that I have you in my life. I thank God everyday that you and I have become best friends.

To Robert Jervey and Vanessa Jervey. Thank both of you for shaping the woman that I was destined to become. Were it not for each of you, in your own right, I would not have persevered and challenged myself to become better, stronger, Incredible.

To Sylvia Waddell, my biggest fan …Aunt Nette, I am so thankful that God saw fit to make you my aunt. Thank you for believing in me so much that I can't help but thank you. You make me smile when I think of the heart of gold that I get to be enclosed in. I love you!

To my Pastor and First Lady, Shannon and Shawnika McNeil of Kingdom Harvest Fellowship. Thank you, Thank you, Thank You. You believed in me and stretched me unconditionally and I thank you! To the entire KHF family, thank you.

To Nina Parker. Girl. I am praising the Lord for you. You are an angel and I am so blessed to have someone like you believe in me. Because of you, I can dance. You are the wind beneath my wings and even though I may not tell you daily, always know that I love you beyond words, thoughts and limits. You are my oldest and dearest friend. I thank God for you!

To Sharon Homer. You are such an important part of my life. Thank you. 2009 is your year to bear fruit. Have you made room for your produce stand yet?

To Tonja Jennings. My photographer and friend. Girl, you keep me looking good. Thank you for taking the pictures that are empowering the world.

To Tara Taylor. Although I have known you for such a short time, you have made an Incredible impact on my life. Thank you for consistently offering of yourself unselfishly to help me to live my dream.

To Pastor Monica Haskell and my MPACT Sisters! I praise God for MPACT and the vision cultivated by Pastor Monica. Your coaching has been invaluable. Thank you!

The Incredible You

Unleash the Incredible You; a you, bursting with Passion, Abundance, Confidence and Expectation:

Principle 1. Trust that God has your best interests at heart.
Principle 2. Have a heart that is ready to serve others.
Principle 3. Experience life through eyes of faith.
Principle 4. In all things, be grateful. Have an attitude of gratitude, it will overflow your cup.
Principle 5. Never give up on yourself no matter what others may say.
Principle 6. Create a life where everything is in proper balance and perspective.
Principle 7. Release yourself from the issues, hurts and struggles of your past.
Principle 8. Expect unmerited favor in your life.
Principle 9. Decide that vision is your key to victory.
Principle 10. Increase your self-image.
Principle 11. Be Happy.
Principle 12. Live to love.
Principle 13. Execute your goals and dreams with enthusiastic expectation.
Principle 14. You already possess the keys to the Incredible You, believe it!
Principle 15. Offer yourself the opportunity to overcome obstacles and adversity with passion and promise.
Principle 16. Unleash the promises for an Incredible You!

Other Books by Darnyelle A. Jervey

*If You Understood My Past,
You Would Understand My Praise*

Dream the Incredible, the Journal

Speak the Incredible

Maximizing the Incredible You

Burn the Box: 50 Ways to Eliminate Excuses, Facilitate Change and Overcome Adversity in Life & Business

All books are available at www.amazon.com or www.incredibleoneenterprises.com

Hello, Incredible One!

I want to welcome you to ***The Incredible You: Unleash Passion, Abundance, Confidence and Expectation in Your Life***. My mission is clear: to help you to define and unleash the Incredible You! But more importantly, to define the Incredible You using spiritual and scriptural references.

You may ask why I am using the Bible to define the Incredible You? The reason is simple. Regardless of what you call your higher source, whether you even acknowledge Him or not, He exists and through his creation of the abundant universe in which we live, we are given the power and authority to live the Incredible life we were created to enjoy. Because I am the author of this book and my higher source is the one true and living God, I will refer to Him, His word and ordinances as it relates to the spiritual laws governing your life and the universe.

Whether you have a personal relationship with Him or not, your birth was predestined when He created the world and He made you and me in His Incredible image. It is not my desire to convince you to believe what I believe; but because I believe that if you want to lead, you must read and my absolute favorite book is the Bible, I will be using it as an illustration of the principles I outline in this book.

Do you feel Incredible?

Do you want to define the Incredible You? If so, I invite you to allow God to inhabit your life. When you let Him in, He will replace doubt, fear, debt and discouragement with prosperity, a positive attitude, passion and most importantly peace. Trust me; the Incredible You wants to live in peace.

Are you ready to start your journey toward becoming Incredible? If so, please take this journey with me and allow the Bible to minister to you so that you realize that you are already Incredible.

This book doubles as an interactive guide, at the end of each chapter questions will be asked of you to instill self-reflection using the PACE method developed by Incredible One Enterprises, LLC.

Self-reflection is an important part of your development and I invite you to take it seriously. When I began to reflect, my life changed immensely.

The PACE method is defined as follows:
P – Plan with purposeful **passion**.
A – Achieve with an attitude of **abundance**.
C – Create with consistent **confidence**.
E – Execute with enthusiastic **expectation**.

Plan to Achieve by Creating then Executing in the areas of Passion, Abundance, Confidence and Expectation. All people who have ever been successful in life have these four things in common and so I created the PACE Method My goal is to impart the tools in your life to allow you to become intentional about the life you are creating. The universe will support your creation when you begin to unleash the Incredible and speak what you seek.

From mind to motion, these action steps will enact Incredible change in your life.

This book should not be a substitution for a journal. If you do not currently use journaling as a practice of self-reflection and personal development, I strongly encourage you to start. Trust me; journaling will be a blessing to your soul. The journal I offer, *Dream the Incredible Journal*, is a great companion to this book!

The Incredible You is about making a transition. We are moving from the old you to the new you. The new you is Incredible!

Can I be honest with you? I mean, really honest. In this book, I pour out my heart to you. I share the lessons I've learned that have allowed me to declare myself Incredible. I'm not being cocky or conceited when I say that I realize that I possess every key I need to open every door to my destiny and if you take the time to read this book and answer the questions with honesty and authenticity, you will too. I guarantee it.

Because I was honest with myself when I completed my first self-assessment, I was able to turn my breakdown into a breakthrough and change the course of my life forever.

I invite you to define and unleash the Incredible you.
My favorite book says that life and death lie in the power of the tongue. We bring about those things that we speak about after we have first thought about them. Because it is your mission to be Incredible, you must start speaking about the Incredible You; you must speak life to your life. You must be intentional and specific about what you allow to proceed out of your mouth. Each word is heard by the universe and the universe must give you what you ask it for. It's the law. When you guard your mouth, you guard your life. You must learn to speak what you have so that it will come to pass. You want wealth, health and prosperity? Speak it. You want a great marriage? Speak it. We cannot just speak amiss; be specific and strategic about the words that you allow to come out of your mouth.

I remember when I was little, always hearing adults say 'if you don't have anything nice to say, you shouldn't say anything at all.' Well, when it comes to defining and unleashing the Incredible You, I agree. If you don't have anything nice to say about who you are, stop where you are and don't say anything. Mute your tongue so that you don't kill yourself with your words. Without even realizing it, we make casual covenants encouraging us to live in fear, doubt, disgust and dysfunction. Control your tongue and guard your mind, it will lead to the Incredible You.

We all suffer with a wandering mind. Even the United Negro College Fund is noted for saying that "a mind is a terrible thing to waste." My favorite book says "as a man thinks, so is he." Again, your mind is the focus of this phrase. The mind is a dangerous thing when left to conclude matters on its own. You must prevent yourself from speaking what you think as it may kill you. It will not start as a literal death but if left untreated, it can lead to the doubt, discouragement and depression that can result in a physical death.

What does it mean to control the power of your tongue and allow it to let you live a life of abundance? Abundance has very little to do with money, abundance is a state of mind. It means that you will speak life to your life and not cut off your nose to spite your face. It means that you will believe that you can, you will, you must. It means that you realize that you can do anything to which you put your mind. Abundance is your right; God created an abundant universe and each of us is entitled to a portion of that abundance. Mary Kay Ash has been quoted for saying "Whatever the mind can conceive and believe, it can achieve." Conception entails thinking and speaking and from here on out, when you speak, speak life....

When you say things like "I'm broke," "I can't seem to do anything right," or "I am so stupid," you will keep killing your thoughts, hopes and dreams because your belief is not bigger than your fear. Trust me, fear, if left untreated, can be the catalyst of many missed opportunities. F.E.A.R., quite simply, fights every alternative to reality.

We allow fear to placate itself in our lives and allow us to see things that really don't exist just to rationalize why we cannot accomplish our goals and dreams. What I believe is important to point out is that we are all born with two (2) fears: the fear of falling and the fear of loud noise. However, at some point in time in our lives, we embrace more fears and those fears paralyze us and inhibit our ability to do what we were created to do.

But no more, The Incredible You is on the horizon and you must speak life and put yourself in the position to do the impossible.

When you stop allowing fear to prevent you from writing your ticket to success and start walking by faith, the Incredible You will appear out of nowhere.

What does your tongue speak? It is capable of speaking life. Decide today that you will stop existing and start living by speaking one word at a time.

With God's help and through this book, it is my mission to give you some tools to be able to walk into your destiny and get excited, your destiny is INCREDIBLE!

Expansion creates Exposure

Expand your mind and expose yourself to the Incredible You. You can do it; I pray this book helps. Please note that each principle is interdependent, which means that you need to master all of them to define the Incredible You. Life is like Burger King; "you can have it your way" when you commit to doing the work necessary with integrity, discipline, an open heart and willing spirit.

Be Incredible! It's already in you.

The Incredible You: Self-Assessment

As we begin to define the Incredible You, it is important that you take the time for self-reflection. Knowing where you start your journey is essential to coming out of this book different, better, INCREDIBLE.

As I endeavor to share my principles with you, you must be honest with yourself. Honesty and authenticity will help to make the transition easier. It is time to leverage your strengths and face the fear that will most assuredly accompany the journey that you will undertake. It is worth it to expand your mind and never allow it to return to the same place. It is time to take the road less traveled; this journey will make all the difference in your life.

If you are ready….it's time to define

The Incredible You…

The Incredible You
Defined...

Please take a minute and honestly answer the following statements/questions:

Finish this sentence: As I embark on this book, I expect...

_____
_____
_____
_____
_____

The thing from my past which is holding my captive is...

_____
_____
_____
_____
_____

I believe that if I applied myself in the area listed below, I would be Incredible...

_____
_____
_____
_____
_____
_____

Darnyelle A. Jervey

Five words I would use to describe myself are...

_____
_____
_____

My biggest opportunities for personal improvement are...

_____
_____
_____

If every job paid $20 an hour, I would be...

_____
_____
_____

I am better than anyone else in the world at...

_____
_____
_____

I get excited when...

_____
_____
_____
_____

The Incredible You

I am motivated and inspired by…
_____
_____
_____
_____

I am talented when it comes to…
_____
_____
_____
_____

To me, passion means…
_____
_____
_____
_____

I wake up each morning because of …
_____
_____
_____
_____

My favorite things to do include…
_____
_____
_____
_____

What I want out of my life is…

_____
_____
_____
_____

I feed my spirit by…

_____
_____
_____
_____

My definition of abundance is…

_____
_____
_____
_____

I am most confident about…

_____
_____
_____
_____

I am allowing the following to prevent me from walking into my destiny…

_____
_____
_____
_____
_____

The Incredible You

I would describe my life as ...
_____
_____
_____

What I love most about me is...
_____
_____
_____

My personal mission statement is...
_____
_____
_____

My friends would use the following words to describe me...
_____
_____
_____

To become Incredible, I am prepared to...
_____
_____
_____
_____

Darnyelle A. Jervey

I have a positive attitude; be honest! Share why or why not here…

_____
_____
_____

The person who has impacted my life the most is (could be a positive or negative impact, please share why)…

_____
_____
_____
_____

I am grateful for…

_____
_____
_____
_____

True or False: What I am doing right now is getting me closer to where I want to be. Share your thoughts…

_____
_____
_____
_____

I have made a choice to be Incredible starting today because…

_____
_____
_____
_____

Preface

Simply put, being Incredible is the realization that you were born that way. So many of us allow life to beat us down and prevent us from walking into our birthright. We have become so hardened to the possibility that we were created to soar as eagles. Did you know that eagles fly at an altitude where the average bird cannot survive? We have convinced ourselves that we have made our bed and now we have to lie in it. We have decided that we are down for the count; there is no way that we have the strength to get back up again. We have decided to allow the enemy to pounce on us and beat us like we stole something. So we just sit and wallow in our self-pity. Sound familiar?

The only one who can change your situation is you. But not just any you, the Incredible You.

Do you want to live an Incredible Life? Do you desire to be considered Incredible in your own right? Are you ready for this; it will be mind blowing....**The only thing separating you from the Incredible You is yourself, your mindset and your tongue**.

Your mindset is the key to unlocking passion, abundance, confidence and expectation in your life. Get excited, you are only a mind shift away from living a P.A.C.E. life.

Living an Incredible life is much simpler than we all make it seem. An Incredible life is not about the size of your car, house or paycheck. Living an Incredible Life is about the size of your mind. Your mindset, your way of looking at the glass on the table, is the first indication as to if you are capable of living Incredibly. When you operate in lack, your cup is half-empty. When you think positively, your cup is half-full but when and only when you live in abundance does your cup overflow and you actually begin to position yourself as the cup, recognizing that you are in control of your future. You and you alone. Very easily, you can take the lid off of your thinking and move from forgettable to Incredible! Are you ready? I know that you are thinking 'that girl is crazy. She has no idea what I have been through. She makes it sound easy, but I have been to hell and back.' Is that your story?

Well, when are you going to get sick and tired of telling it? When are you going to realize that if you want something you have never had you must become willing to do something that you have never done. Guess what? Why not start now? Is there anything that would keep you from giving finding the Incredible You a try? I didn't think so!

Do you want to change your life and live Incredibly? Get out of the box. Neither you nor God can move when you are boxed in. Once you start living out on the branch, where the fruit of life is, you will notice that every day problems and obstacles no longer become hindrances or stumbling blocks that get in your way and keep you from fulfilling your Incredible life goals and dreams.

The difference between stumbling blocks and stepping stones is how you use them.

Being Incredible has absolutely nothing to do with what others think of you, being Incredible is about self-esteem, self-worth and self-love. See the word self a lot? That's because what other people think about you really and truly is not something with which you should concern yourself. Do you believe that you possess the keys to an Incredible life? I believe you do.

When I was twenty-five years old, the bottom fell out of my life. I felt like I had lost everything because I allowed a man to define my worth. When the dust settled and I began to pick up the pieces of my shattered existence, I realized that I already possessed everything I needed to turn my thought process and mindset around. I was the master of my mind and mediocrity was removed from my vocabulary.

Today, I know that I am living an Incredible Life; I was able to finally write a book about that time in my life. *If You Understood My Past, You Would Understand My Praise* chronicles that part of my life's journey.

But if you understood my past, you would understand why today, helping others define their Incredibleness is so important to me.

What changed? Something simple, I started to believe in myself and I developed a personal relationship with the Lord, giving myself permission to be my best. I allowed the spiritual principles of the universe to give me permission and authority to change my life. I recognized that I am the creator of my life and that the universe supports my efforts to create the life I want. I also stopped being concerned about what other people thought of me and I decided to march to the beat of my own drum. I started making my own music. And now I dance like nobody's watching...

I forgave myself for the past, those wrongs suffered me as well as those wrongs I did to others out of anger, rage or sheer discontentment. I began to dream and think about what I wanted to do with my life whereas before, I wanted what others wanted for me.

My passion was born out of my brokenness and I desired to change my outlook so that I could later help others do the same. As I underwent this transformation, I stumbled upon these self-determined keys to an Incredible life. I now desire to share them with the world.

The keys are simple and indicated on the throughout this book. My goal is to highlight these principles, expand upon them with supporting concepts and offering solutions to make the key changes and mind shifts necessary to help you walk into your Incredibleness. The Incredible You is closer than you think; get ready to walk it out.

Definitions

Incredible – surpassing belief; too extraordinary and improbable to admit of belief; unlikely; marvelous; fabulous

Unleash – to pursue or run at will; to abandon control of

Passion - a strong or extravagant fondness, enthusiasm, or desire for anything

Abundance - an extremely plentiful or over sufficient quantity or supply, overflowing fullness; affluence, wealth

Confidence - belief in oneself and one's powers or abilities; self-confidence; self-reliance; assurance

Expectation - an expectant mental attitude; a prospect of future good or profit

The Incredible You... Principles

Principle One:

*T*RUST THAT GOD HAS YOUR BEST INTERESTS AT HEART.

Trust is such a simple concept. We trust that when we go to bed at night, we will wake up the next morning. We trust that when we go out to start our car, it will start and take us to our destination without issue or fail. We trust that when we leave for work, our home will still be there when we return.

Why then is it so difficult to trust that God has your best interests at heart?

Becoming the Incredible You is contingent on your ability to trust the Creator in all things. The Bible makes it very clear; when we trust Him, He is able to show up in our lives and do supernatural things. Please know that I am talking about relationship, not religion. Just as you trust your spouse or significant other to always consider your best interests, you must give God the same consideration and place in your life. In fact, God should have the most important place in your relationship hierarchy.

When I graduated from college, my first job barely paid me $20,000 a year as a base salary. My finances did not permit me to handle all of my basic needs yet God made a way for all of my needs to be supplied because I trusted Him.

I remember it like it was just the other day, I was twenty-two years old and I had just purchased my first home. When I went to settlement, the seller was supposed to include a refrigerator in the settlement deal; however, when I arrived at my new home, there was no refrigerator and the seller could not be found. My realtor told me that unfortunately because we had not listed the refrigerator as an inclusion on the settlement agreement, we had no legal recourse, which meant that I had a new home, but no way to refrigerate my food.

I was tapped out; I was already living below standard and my paycheck was more like a poor check. So I lived "poor" check to "poor" check and the thought of having one more unplanned expense had me very discouraged. However, I trusted God. In my favorite book, David, the King says, "I was young and now I am old yet I have never seen the righteous forsaken or their children begging bread." So I cried out to the Lord in prayer. I told Him my need and because His Word says that "if we believe, we will receive whatever we ask for in prayer," I trusted that He would make a way. I was too dumb to doubt that He wouldn't make a way for me to get a refrigerator, even though my bank account clearly said otherwise.

As I remember back to that time, I don't know where the calm in my spirit came from, but I was extremely calm. For some reason, I just knew that God had my back and I was content waiting for Him to supply my need. In the meantime, I borrowed a cooler from my parents and got some ice and kept a few items there for my daily needs.

Three days after I moved into my new home, I got a phone call from the Sears Outlet store that they had a refrigerator in my name that had already been paid for. They were calling to make delivery arrangements!

The Incredible You

We serve an Incredible God. I knew that God would not leave me or forsake me. I knew that someway, somehow, I would be a victor, not a victim. Now, I could have easily gotten discouraged and become angry at the seller or even others for getting me into this mess. But I serve a God that is able to do exceedingly, abundantly above all that I could ask or even think! I have decided to trust that God has my best interests at heart.

God knows what is best for me; He knows what is best for you. Just like the hairs on your head are numerous, so are the illustrations of God's undying love for you. I promise you that trusting God truly is the key to a life of abundance.

For all intents of purposes, abundance is not material; it is living above strife, stress and contention. A person who lives in abundance trusts the Lord in all things. Whether in plenty or in want, trusting in God puts your mind and spirit at ease so that you can focus on the things that need to be handled.

God's Word tells us to trust Him in so many places; in fact the word "trust" is used in the Bible 147 times, 44 times alone throughout the Psalms. Not included in this number are all of the times that a variation of the word trust, such as trusted, trustworthy or trusting, is mentioned in the Bible.

When we seek new relationships, whether personal or professional, we determine the viability of the relationship on how much we trust the person or believe that we can trust them. Trust is a sliding scale for most people; one starts with enough to either add to or take away from the fabric of a relationship. Trust is so important; regardless of the relationship, we say that trust must ensue or we want nothing to do with it. I subscribe to you that when it comes to having a relationship with the Lord and living an

Incredible Life, it is more important than ever that your trust lies in the knowledge that He has your best interests at heart.

We struggle with putting our trust in God because we would rather put our confidence in man. My favorite book warns us that "it is better to trust in the Lord than to put confidence in man." Trust me, I have been there, done that and gotten a t-shirt for all the times that I put my confidence in man. Man always costs me; however, a personal relationship with God is free! The surprising thing is that when man lets me down, it is God that builds me back up. As a result, I have learned to skip the middleman and get right to trusting God in all circumstances. It wasn't easy, but through getting to know Christ for myself, I was able to let Him have His way. He knows better than I.

I know what you are thinking, "I can see man at work, but God doesn't come when I need Him." Better still, I know that you are sick and tired of the old cliché: "He may not come when you want Him but He is always right on time," right? But God is in control and He is going to have His way with or without your consent! Trust me when I tell you to trust God and let Him have His way. It is a win-win situation because when He has His way, you will ultimately have yours, trust me!

I have had more than a few instances when I had to remember that not now doesn't mean never. "Delayed does not mean denied." With God in control, there will always be a time and place that is much better.

To those people who know me, it's no surprise that I am choosing to share this as I talk about the importance of trusting the Lord and trusting that He has your best interests at heart. I have been engaged twice. Once a source of great embarrassment for me, especially the first time, today I get excited because I would rather say "yes" to the wrong man, and then realize it before the altar than to not get the realization and block my blessings and throw off my destiny.

Do I desire to be married? Absolutely! Is it so important that I am willing to settle and trust myself rather than God? Absolutely not! As I say, I have been there, done that and gotten the t-shirt. Because I trust God, I am not willing to settle. More importantly, I am not willing to trust myself solely with this very important decision. My favorite book makes it clear that when we seek Him first, He is able to add everything that we need to our lives. I trust and believe that when He sees fit, the right man of God will present himself and find me, the key to his favor! And, according to a story in my favorite book, he will wake up and realize with me in his life, his destiny can now be fulfilled.

When we are growing up, we trust that our parents know what is best for us. As we grow and mature, we feel confident that we have learned what is best for us and we no longer need to rely on our parents. I submit to you that at all times, God knows what is best for you. He tells us in Jeremiah 1:5 that He knew us before we were even formed in our mother's womb and even then, He established a trust pact with us that He would never leave us or forsake us. (Deuteronomy 31:6)

Sometimes the pain in your life will make you feel like peace, calm, belief, confidence and strength seem so far away, but trust God. To empower and impact change in your life, you must become a F.R.O.G. and Fully Rely On God or trust Him to do what He says He will do. Psalm 37 is a powerful psalm of David talking about the importance of trusting in the Lord. When you as Psalm 37:5 says commit your way to the Lord and trust in Him, He will make your life Incredible!

Wisdom from my favorite book:
Commit your way to the Lord, trust in him and he will do this.

Note: Please write the answers to each question in your Dream the Incredible Journal. It will allow you to chronicle your journey to becoming the Incredible You.

Unleash
Passion Abundance Confidence Expectation
Food for thought: Trusting God with the PACE Method.

Planning with Purposeful Passion:
What can you do today to illustrate that you trust God with all your heart? Write down some examples of how you plan to TRUST God so that your life is filled with purposeful passion.

Achieving with an Attitude of Abundance:
How can you achieve an abundant attitude about putting all of your trust in God? When other people interact with you, are they able to see abundance in action? Can you honestly attribute the abundance you seek to your ability to be a FROG? Why or Why not?

Creating with Consistent Confidence:
What would it mean in your life if you were able to create situations to TRUST God with consistent confidence? Is it hard for you to trust God with consistent confidence? Why or Why not? Do you have TRUST issues? What are you prepared to do to impact a change in this area?

Executing with Enthusiastic Expectation:
What steps are you going to take to execute your TRUST in God while ensuring that you are expecting an enthusiastic experience? What does enthusiasm mean to you? What does it mean to expect something? What do you expect as a result of taking this personal journey?

Principle Two:

HAVE A HEART THAT IS READY TO SERVE OTHERS.

Service must be each and every one of our goals. We must realize it is not about us. Marianne Williamson in her famous poem "Our Deepest Fear" says that "when we let our light shine, we unconsciously give others permission to do the same." Letting your light shine is about having a heart to serve others. If you want to live in your P.A.C.E., it is absolutely essential that you have a heart that is ready to serve others.

I will be the first to admit that this was a tough one for me. For so long, the pleasures of life had been denied me so when I finally got a chance to "do me," I did me big. So big in fact that it was as if nothing or no one else mattered. Big mistake. I came from the "if you want something done right do it yourself" breed of women. My parents taught me that lesson the hard way; as a result, it was truly the grace and love of God that made me realize that my way was not the right way to do things.

Because I had suffered so many hurts, I didn't believe that there was anyone out there who had genuine concern for me, which gave me a hardened heart. Because I knew I could do it right, it went straight to my head. And I relied on me to make things happen, a big mistake.

I realized not too long ago that what we do for others is what makes us Incredible. A self-less lifestyle gives me a personal joy that cannot be fulfilled in any other way. It's not about me; it's not about you. It's about making others feel Incredible. I personally have declared that every person has a stamp on his or her forehead, which says, "Make Me Feel Incredible." That means smiling and saying "hello" to people who cross your path. That means offering a compliment when you think it, as you may have the personal power to change someone's day. Moreover, thinking about others will add such an Incredible impact to your own life.

We cannot receive what God wants to do in us if we are selfish and focus only on our own desires; we must be willing to get out and do for others. Whether that is in the form of volunteering in our churches, the community, being a Big Brother or Sister, donating time to read to children or seniors, it doesn't matter, please just get out and share yourself shamelessly so that someone else might be enriched because of you.

I believe that the true measure of a man is by how much of himself he gives to others. You should give the good things about yourself away everyday. There are lots of people and organizations who need the help that you can offer to their organization. As an example, I am a motivational speaker. I have volunteered to speak at non-profit organizations and community centers to help others, those who are less fortunate, hear an inspiring message. I share my story so that someone might be blessed by realizing that they too can achieve success.

As you may or may not know, my mother was incarcerated when I was a young girl. Each of us has a story and each of us have more baggage than you can ever take on an airplane. Moreover, when you are able to get your baggage down to a carry on, it is time to help someone else do the same. The belief and love that you share selflessly with others may be just what they need to get their lives together.

As a result of being able to overcome the devastation of being without my mother during my important years, a cause that has become near and dear to my heart is mentoring other little girls who are experiencing the same things. Someone may have thought that because I come from parents who were in jail and addicted to drugs, I could not surmount the odds and impact change in the lives of others. But I did. I am. I was blessed with the favor of God to rise above my circumstances and it is my mission to help other children and teenagers learn that they can do the same.

You only need one person to go before you to break a belief barrier. Similarly, right now as I write this in 2008, we have witnessed history in our election of the next President of the United States of America. Barack Obama, the son of an African man, successfully secured the Democratic nomination for this prestigious position. I am sure that at some point in time when Barack was a little boy someone told him that he could never be the President of the United States. I am also sure that someone else poured into him and breathed belief so that he would realize that he could dream the impossible and do Incredible things! Today, little African-American boys and girls everywhere are now able to see the invisible and dream the Incredible because of President Elect Obama and all the rest of the people who have gone before us and broken significant belief barriers. I know it warms my heart to know that I am possible.

Eight years ago, he was not able to get into the Democratic National Convention because he did not have the necessary credentials. Four years ago, he was asked to speak at the Convention. Two years ago, he announced his candidacy for the President of the United States of America. As of November 2008, he is the President Elect! Today, as you read this book, we have elected our first Black President. Incredible things will happen when you realize that you are Incredible because you have a heart determined to serve others!

What God says about you is true whether or not other people believe or validate it. God said that Barack would deliver our nation from the stress that it is currently experiencing just as God did in the Bible days when He sent Barak (same name, different spelling,) and Deborah to deliver His people in Judges Chapter 4. God said that Barack is powerful beyond measure. God said that he would be the best man for the job. Even if you didn't vote for him, you will call him President Obama. He is Incredible!

President Elect Obama is known for his servant leadership style. Even as he gave his President-Elect speech, that servant mentality was alive and well. As he so eloquently shared his plans for a new America, he shared those plans with a servant attitude and from a servant leadership perspective.

Mary Kay Ash is quoted for saying a variation of a truth from my favorite book: "What you send into the lives of others is most undoubtedly coming back into that of your own," or what we know to be "what you sow you shall reap." No matter how you slice it, you have to send joy to reap joy. When joy is your goal, you will gain growth for yourself as well as show love to someone else. Remember that my favorite book says "There is no greater love than a man who would lay down his life for a friend." Don't you want to be recognized for having a heart of service?

I am sure that your job has some sort of Community Reinvestment Act where you go out and serve in the community. When I worked in Corporate America, we had several choices. Maybe it is becoming a mentor or working with the youth in your church. It is not about you, it is about perpetuating the love of God. You may be the only Bible that others may read. Will they be drawn to discover their Incredibleness because of the model you set? Or will they say, I thought he/she was a mentor, community leader or Christian?

Jesus washing the disciples' feet is a well-recorded example of servant leadership. Many Pastors and congregations follow this servant leadership model across the world, especially during the Easter holiday season. He becomes the ultimate servant by illustrating the need to be humble and concerned about the welfare of others.

What I know to be true is that service is a form of godliness and since inheriting the kingdom is our goal, I can't think of a better way to get close to God and to become Incredible!

But I challenge you; do not wait until Easter to insert servant leadership into your life, doing it now will define the Incredible You.

Let me also add that service doesn't mean volunteerism. When I go to my favorite restaurant, they serve me yet, they bring me a bill. In fact, it is a disservice to not value your contribution to others.

Wisdom from my favorite book:
Just as the Son of Man did not come to be served, but to serve, and to give his life as a ransom for many.

Unleash
Passion Abundance Confidence Expectation
Food for thought: Serving others with the PACE Method.

Planning with Purposeful Passion:
What can you plan to do today that will help you to be a better servant? How do you already illustrate servant hood in your life? What activities are you passionate about? Can you share them with others to help them to develop a similar passion?

Achieving with an Abundant Attitude:
What will serving others do for your attitude? What is the best way to gain an abundance mentality when thinking of serving others? How can you exercise abundance in your life and achieve fulfillment while you also help to define someone else?

Creating with Consistent Confidence:
What can you create in your life today that coincides with your goal to serve others? How can instilling confidence in the dreams of someone else via volunteering also bring confidence consistently into your life?

Execute with Enthusiastic Expectation:
What can you do differently NOW to ensure an enthusiastic expectation for everyone involved? What do you expect to change in your life when you start (or enhance) serving others? What is your execution plan for having a heart to serve?

Principle Three:

*E*XPERIENCE LIFE THROUGH EYES OF FAITH.

I absolutely love this premise. It is a personal favorite. It is from this principle that I decided that I can, I will and I must become a faith giant. In order to aid my development in this area, I created my personal mantra: "If I can see the invisible, God can do the impossible so I have permission to dream the Incredible." This mantra is so powerful and I have passed it on to those who have heard me speak, listen to my hotline or listen to my Blog Talk Radio show.

But it is only powerful if you believe. Do you? It is essential to the Incredible You that you develop eyes of faith, eyes that see the invisible and allow you to experience a life full of limited fears and worries.

Are you excited just thinking about it?

To become the Incredible You, it is unequivocally important that you allow yourself to see life through eyes of faith. Faith produces your ability to work hard and know in your heart that the best is yet to come your way. Now, let's be clear. Faith is amazing when the truth of the condition is within your power to believe. But faith requires action and should honestly be considered a verb.

For example, let's say that you desire to have your own bakery one day. Okay, just play along so I can prove my point. You are believing that it will happen. Something in your spirit gets excited and warm and fuzzy about the thought having a business that was created out of the passion that rests in your bosom. You have faith that one day it will happen. That is awesome.

Faith is what gets the party started. But in order for life to be experienced through eyes of faith, you must act on your faith. What I mean is that you cannot just believe that you will have a bakery yet everyday when you get off of work, you come home and plop down on your leather couch. Faith is an action; it will not work properly if nothing changes in your mind, thought process and daily duties to make the faith a reality. If year after year, you keep believing that you will own a bakery one day but year after year you do nothing to make it happen, your faith is not being exercised. The Incredible You must take action and work each day to bring those ideas, goals, dreams, qualities and characteristics into the reality of your existence. After all, you know that faith without works is dead and we've already decided that the Incredible You was going to only speak life.

Let's examine my mantra statement. If you can see the invisible (that's the faith part.) If you can expand your vision beyond what eyes can see, if you are able to see those things that do not yet exist and get excited about them, you will be able to allow God (the universe) to perform Incredible things in your life. He will be able to do those things deemed impossible by man. Most importantly, you will be an active participant of a dream that is Incredible and you will know that the Incredible is not only possible, but that it will become a reality.

Living through eyes of faith is the only way to live. Trust me. Looking over your shoulder in doubt is no way to move through this life. Again, I have been there, done that and gotten the t-shirt. Remember, God sent His only begotten son so that you might have a life of abundance. How are you supposed to have a life of abundance if you are living in fear? You will hear me say this a lot when it comes to developing the Incredible You: fear has got to go.

Remember, fear, quite simply is false evidence appearing real. Think about it. Something or someone leads you to believe that the thing you are afraid of is the truth and as real as you or me. As a real life example, let's say you are afraid of spiders. They can be scary. Your fear for them perplexes you and handicaps you when they cross your path. But let's break it down. Can a spider overpower you and cause the harm that you allow your mind to tell you it can? Of course not, you can quite simply dismantle a spider and prevent him from spinning his web, as that is the most dangerous thing he will likely do - at least the kind of spiders that we see in everyday life. He can't harm you at all. But the fear leads you to believe or appears by way of reality to lead you to believe that harm is coming your way. That is a lie from the pit! But we get all discombobulated when we see one, don't we?

If you want to unleash the Incredible You, you must stop allowing fear to immobilize and hinder you from walking toward and into those things that you want. It is possible, when you remember that God did not give you a spirit of fear. Fear is not of God.

Moreover, fear and faith cannot occupy the same space. It is not possible that you can be sure and doubt at the same time. Think about it. Is it possible? Of course it's not! So why do we let fear talk us out or defraud us from achieving our goals and dreams?

I remember the time when I was trying to decide if I would leave my secure job and go out on my own. I was no longer fulfilled in my Corporate America career. I started to get headaches while driving into the parking lot at work. It was a high stress environment and I was no longer making a difference. I had topped out as far as I wanted to

The Incredible You

---

go there because it wasn't my passion. It was a chore just to get up every morning. Sound familiar? But for years after I was no longer fulfilled, I went everyday because it paid the bills.

How many of you are living beneath your privilege today because you are afraid of how the bills will be paid? It's okay, I was once there too.

Back to the story, while I was doing an excellent job for my employer each day, it was no longer what brought me joy. I was sure of one thing – God did not call me to do that – giving a half attempt at doing my job without excitement, passion and enthusiasm. I heard God clearly tell me that the time had come for me to leave my job and start my own business. I had faith that God would make a way yet I was also afraid of failure so I didn't move. I was disobedient. I stayed where I was, miserable.

I became angry with God and tried to understand why He would have me in a situation where I couldn't thrive. Yet, it wasn't God's fault. I had blatantly disobeyed His command for my life. As a result of my disobedience, my departure was delayed by another year and a half. Do you know what I lost in that time? I lost key components of me! And, I can never get that time back. Because of God's grace, the lost time only slowed me down. Delay is not denial. My destiny was still fulfilled. I am walking in it each day.

What's my point? Trust God, the first principle in becoming the Incredible You. You must move when He says move. Just like that. Without question. It may be scary and you may be shaking in your boots but if you delight yourself in Him (or obey) He will give you the desires of your heart. That's what He says in His Word and since He is not a man and He has no reason to lie to you or me, I feel confident in telling you to trust and believe Him.

I did finally step out on faith and start my own company. God did still bless me like He promised to do. But because I did not directly align myself with His timing, I lost some things in the shuffle. I would never want for you to do that. Instead, I would want you to be fulfilled and enjoy all the rewards that come with trusting in God.

One of my favorite songs is by Smokie Norful, "I Know Too Much About Him." I love this song because the words are so true. Just like no one can tell you that your name isn't your name, no one should be able to tell you that God can fail. The truth is that He can't. When you know too much about Him, you won't be able to doubt Him and the dreams and goals He places in your heart. Fear is just doubt and disbelief. When you have eyes of faith, when you see those things that are not as though they are, you can truly live. There will be nothing binding you to failure or fear. The Incredible You will be waiting.

Wisdom from my favorite book:
And it is written: eye hath not seen, nor ear heard, nor entered into the heart of man that which God has for him who loves him.

Unleash
Passion Abundance Confidence Expectation

Food for thought: Developing eyes of faith using the PACE Method.

Planning with Purposeful Passion:
What makes you afraid? What is keeping you from becoming a FROG and fully relying on God to develop your faith? What does faith mean to you? What can you do now that will help you to turn your fear into faith? What would your life look like if you experienced it through eyes of faith?

Achieving with an Attitude of Abundance:
What is your personal definition of abundance? What is your attitude about living? Are you living or existing? Explain. What can you begin to do today to build toward an attitude of abundance especially in the area of faith?

Creating with Consistent Confidence:
What can you began to create in your life today that will lead to developing the confidence to know that your eyes will allow you to see things in faith? What did you write in your journal today?

Executing with Enthusiastic Expectation:
Now that you've set your plan to achieve eyes of faith with confidence, what will you do to make it happen? Remember faith without works is dead!

Principle Four:

*I*N ALL THINGS, BE THANKFUL, AN ATTITUDE OF GRATITUDE OVERFLOWS YOUR CUP.

Gratitude is realizing that it is not all about you; gratitude keeps you humble. To define the Incredible You, you have got to know that it's not about you. What you do for others is what defines you and adds depth to your character. Sure, we can all be self-centered and get along just fine but we will not be happy because we will not have anyone but ourselves. Take it from me, I've been there, done that and gotten the souvenir t-shirt.

I remember vividly about my personal path to destruction, which occurred just after I graduated from high school. I was always an angry person and I took everything for granted. I felt like the world owed me something because I had been abused and because my mother had gone to jail and abandoned me. I had a major chip on my shoulder and in my mind, it was all about Darnyelle. No one else mattered. In my self-absorbed stupor, I missed out on so much. There were so many people who wanted to help me and believe in me but my "Oscar the Grouch" routine chased them away. At the end of the day, when it was all said and done, I was not Incredible. I was laughable. I had nothing and I had no one.

Sometimes I laugh when I recall those scenarios since I have become a better person of when people make comments like, "I didn't really like you when I met you. There was something about you that rubbed me the wrong way. But now that I have gotten to know you, you are not that bad." I chuckle because I was not a good person and although I've been changed, some people still remember the not so nice me. For those who are willing to meet the Incredible me, God bless you. For those who aren't, you've just missed out. Even the Bible says "let he who is without sin cast the first stone," yet no one moved.

What I have learned as a result of my attitude is that everything is based on your way of looking at that glass on the table. If your glass is half-empty, I pray that this book will help you to turn your stinkin' thinkin' off and clean up your act. If you never embrace a positive attitude, you will never meet the Incredible You.

When you do not have an attitude of gratitude and a heart to serve others, you may think people can't smell your funk, but they can and it is sending off signals that say "don't trust him/her. He/She's really not worth the trouble." No matter what is going on, you must have an attitude of gratitude. I am grateful that I woke up this morning. I am grateful that I am able to walk. I am grateful that I have soap to wash my body. I am grateful that I can find multiple clothing options in my closet. I am grateful that I can start my car and there is gas in it.

When you operate in gratitude no matter what is going on, you will receive release. As we've heard it said, when the blessings go up, the blessings come down. We must pay homage in gratitude for everything that we have. You will not get more if you cannot appreciate what you already have. More importantly, He inhabits the praises of His people. A life where God is your constant keynote speaker is an Incredible life!

Do you have a gratitude journal?

Do you thank the Creator everyday for the little and big things that you are grateful for in your life?

Whenever there are bad things going on, there are also good things going on. A really good friend of mine, Nina Parker, told me something really profound one day, she said "When the best times of your life are happening at the same time as the worst times of your life, you ought to be grateful because God is about to do an Incredible work in you." For example, I was starting my company (a great time) and ending my second engagement (a worst time) at the same time. I was so confused because I thought that God had ear marked that man for me.

What I learned, was that he was a good man, just not a good one for me. It was hard being engaged again and going through all of the excitement of planning a wedding only to have to tell everyone AGAIN, that I had made a mistake and would not be getting married. Now, I am sure that you are saying 'it's better that you found out before you got married,' but it didn't feel better. I had been dating and said 'yes I will' to a wolf in sheep's clothing and the knowledge of that while transitioning from my successful Mary Kay career to my new business was all that I could take. I thought I would break. But God. Because of my best times and worst times colliding, I have experienced exponential spiritual growth. I know that you can get excited about that. It makes me excited every time I think about it.

If you want to live an Incredible Life, you must be grateful in all things. *All things.*

Is your glass half-full or half-empty? Your attitude about life determines how much is in your cup. No matter what comes my way, I am happy. My cup is full. It wasn't always that way, but today, I am so pleased to share with you that it is.

If I took the time to share my latest testimony of trials and tribulations, you would think I was making it up. I mean seriously. But regardless of what is going on in my life, I have joy. In my Incredibleness, I have found that peace that passes all understanding and that is why I am Incredible!

When I started to realize that I lived in the peace of God, wow, my life really began. It doesn't matter what is going on, I am happy and joy surrounds me all the days of my life. Even when things don't go my way, I still have to give it up in thanks and praise to my Father in Heaven because He has held it down for me.

You wouldn't believe the year I have had. 2008, the year of new beginnings, has been a lot of things, a lot of new beginnings in my life. But not exciting ones like you might think, ones that would tear me down and force me to hide under my bed if I didn't practice those keys that I have shared so far: Trust. Heart of Service. Eyes of Faith. All of them contribute to my ability to give thanks in all things. I want to help you do the same.

I've lost cars, income, success (as defined by man), popularity, relationships, loved ones - personal and professional, customers, and income in 2008. But I am still grateful because every need is met and I am yet alive. I have not missed a meal, had a bill go unpaid or struggled with depression.

I am Incredible! All those things were just that, things. They have no bearing on who I am and what I know that I am to become. I know it's an old cliche' but the joy I have, the world didn't give it to me and therefore, the world cannot take it away. I have an attitude of gratitude and that makes me Incredible.

I dare you to try it. Take my challenge. Buy the *Dream the Incredible Journal* and for twenty-one days, right down everything for which you are grateful. I promise you by the twenty-first day, your outlook on life will change and you will realize that so many things don't matter when your mind is aligned with a proper perspective. Remember, expansion creates exposure. Expand your mind and the rest will follow.

Much like God promises to give us peace that passes all understanding, that is what being the Incredible You is all about. It's about realizing that you are just a mind shift away from your Incredibleness.

Always keep in mind that 95% of everything we do is attitude. You've heard the saying, 'you can do everything right with the wrong attitude and fail or everything wrong with the right attitude and succeed?' Which do you prefer? Of course I know the answer and so do you.

My point? Attitude is very important to becoming the Incredible You. We put a lot of stock in it because 95% of what you do everyday, is a lot. Doing things you don't want to do but doing it anyway with a great disposition will blow your mind and open your eyes to all of the possibilities of what God wants to do in you. Are you excited?

Just think, everything will get better when your attitude is right. I am excited for you. It may not always be easy. You know us, especially women; we love our attitudes and PMS moments. But even during those "women" moments, you can stay on track if you remember that God deserves to be thanked at all times.

I encourage you to change your definition of PMS to prayer, meditation and serenity. When your attitude is focused on those things which are ahead of you, you will forget about everything else. You have to learn how to be thankful no matter what is happening around you.

Right now, our country is experiencing an economic shift that will change the livelihood of many people. But you can choose to subscribe to what economists are saying

The Incredible You

about the world's financial systems or you can subscribe to the economy of God. In doing so, you will realize that there is nothing too hard for God. There are plenty of reasons to have an attitude of gratitude.

I love the song "Grateful" by Hezekiah Walker because it sums it all up. We must be grateful for all the things He has done: all the victories, trials, triumphs, successes and even failures that we have experienced in our lives. Gratefulness must flow from your heart and when it does, none of those things will matter.

Decide right now that you will start each day in five (5) minutes of gratitude. Take the time to celebrate what you have and experience in your life right now. When you start each day in gratitude, you are unlocking the possibility of abundance going forward. You will not get more until you are grateful for what you have at this time. Get an attitude of gratitude. It will fill your cup and make you Incredible. I promise.

Wisdom from my favorite book:
In everything give thanks.

Unleash
Passion Abundance Confidence Expectation
Food for thought: Being grateful using the PACE Method.

Planning with Purposeful Passion:
Purchase a journal to record that for which you are grateful. What are you grateful for today? How do you plan to demonstrate this for God, family and coworkers everyday? What do you think always being thankful will do for your passion level in life?

Note: I recommend that before you allow your feet to hit the floor each morning that you express at least five things that you are grateful for. It will set the PACE for your entire day.

Achieving with an Attitude of Abundance:
If you commit to a gratitude journal, what do you think your attitude will become? How quickly will you start to see significant changes in your life because your attitude has been adjusted?

Creating with Consistent Confidence:
What will an attitude of gratitude create in your personal life? At work? At home? What, if anything, makes you resistant to the idea of creating an attitude of gratitude?

Executing with Enthusiastic Expectation:
Now that you've set your plan to have an attitude of gratitude, what will you do to make it happen? List your execution plan here.

Principle Five:

*N*EVER GIVE UP ON YOURSELF DESPITE WHAT OTHERS SAY OR DO.

Want to be Incredible? Stop listening to what others have to say about you. It does not matter what man says, it matters what God says and what you say about yourself. You are who you say you are. Who do you say you are?

It is so important to affirm yourself, and I believe that we should affirm ourselves daily. What do I mean by affirm? I mean, making power statements, faith confessions and every type of statement that speaks life to your life. These statements include: "I am fearfully and wonderfully made," "I am the head and not the tail," "I can do all things through Christ who strengthens me," "I am successful and my dreams are fulfilled," I walk in my purpose each day, "I am powerful beyond measure." When you speak powerful affirmations over yourself and your life, there will naturally be more pep in your step and a desire to fulfill the words you have spoken. It's no secret, no pun intended, that the secret of an Incredible life is to speak what you seek!

Declaration is the key to self-belief. Speak what you want to receive in your life and watch how your desire to give up changes. Try it; I dare you. When you speak and believe life, you will never give up on yourself. I believe that harnessing the power of your tongue is a gift. You will always know that behind the next corner something special exists.

As a child, I never gave in to the words of haters and naysayers when they told me that I couldn't do those things I believed in my heart. I wanted to be more than my situation and I spoke faith confessions over myself to ensure that I would work hard and move beyond my comfort zone to achieve those things. More importantly, I turned my "haters" into reasons to motivate myself to be better, do better and perform better.

There are two basic categories of people in this world. The first are Incredible snatchers, which can be defined by haters, naysayers and dream stealers. These people don't want anything good to come out of your existence. They have been sent to negate all talent and confidence that has been earmarked and reserved for your success. No matter how brilliant the idea, they will talk you down because they cannot stand the thought that you might do something better than them. When you come into contact with these kinds of people, "run Forrest run!"

Unfortunately, these people are typically comprised of those we see most often and to whom we have a blood tie. You've got it; these people are typically your family and "best" friends. Hopefully you are nodding in agreement and simultaneously thinking why do I let them affect me the way that they do? Because they are family and friends and you have a heart. It is essential that you learn how to let their comments roll off your back without ever penetrating the surface of your mind, will or emotions. Simply put, do your best to ignore them! It may not always be easy; but it is key to your survival and becoming the Incredible You.

The second type of people are who I like to call in your Incredible corner. These are the ones who always want the

The Incredible You

best for you and build you up no matter what. You can call these people at any time and ask them for anything and within minutes, it is yours. These people have your back and you can always count on them to be there to assist you in any way possible. They are your brand builders. They are your dream team. They are your biggest cheerleaders. They are your "Amen Corner." You definitely need to foster these relationships and ensure that you are grateful and appreciative of all that they bring to your table.

Who makes up your circle of influence? Are you attracting the Incredible? If you want to be Incredible, it is imperative that you surround yourself with Incredible people. Please do not take this lightly; the people that you allow into your space have a profound affect on who you are and will become. If your goal is to be Incredible, and I assume that it is because you are reading this book, you need to spend time with Incredible people. Do you have a mentor or a success coach? If not, you may want to consider getting one. Consider Darnyelle Jervey, I hear she is Incredible and she has openings! (smile) In order to never give up no matter what others say about you, you need someone powerful to look up to and consult about your dreams, ideas and goals.

On my mother's side of the family, I have seven brothers and sisters. Out of all of them, I am the only one to achieve a high school diploma, undergraduate degree and master's degree. We all came from the same place. Some of us were shackled to the struggle that nothing better existed. Some of us believed that dreaming was a waste of time. Some of us thought that where we came from would always be where we lived. Why was I different? Because I knew that no matter what others had to say, I was destined for greatness. I developed tunnel vision to get to my destination. I got an education and I started to read books and fuel my spirit with the words, thoughts and beliefs that would become my way of life.

Have you always felt that people would know you someday? That you would be a star? I know how you feel and I implore you to decide right now by making a non-negotiable decision that no matter what others have to say, you will work diligently toward your goal.

Sure, there were times when I felt like the world was on top of me. But because I had hidden words of power and learned how to hide the Word of God in my heart, I knew where to turn to get relief. When I needed strength, I knew exactly where to go to get the resolve I needed to keep it moving and you can do the same.

When you were born you were given everything that you need to be Incredible. You don't need to be taller, shorter, thinner, fatter or prettier. You are already Incredible. You must start to believe it, think it, speak it and act like it. Believe what the Bible says about you. Believe what you think about yourself. What I mean is that most of us want to be greater than our station but we start to look around and convince ourselves that it's not possible. We start to listen to what the naysayers have to say and we start to believe that they are correct: we are who we are and who we are is not the person we desire to be. Not So! You can change your station in life by expanding your mind.

Expansion will create the exposure you need to believe that the best is yet to come in your life. When your mind has shifted, it cannot, or should I say, should not, return to the same place. Think about it; let's take flying in an airplane as an example. You are use to flying coach and it is no big deal. But on one trip, you are randomly selected for a free upgrade to First Class – and everything changes. Because your mind has now visualized and experienced the best there is in air transportation and all of the amenities

The Incredible You

that go along with First Class, you mind has expanded, and you no longer want to fly coach because that expansion has exposed you to a new place, another level and a place where you want to spend significant time.

How do you get exposure? Reading books that will feed your mind and spirit and there are many, make sure your list includes the Bible. Regardless of your religious affiliation, if you even have one, the Bible speaks the truth and there is not any situation in this life that has not dealt with in the leather bound cover that keeps everything together.

I have a reading list that I recommend to my coaching clients that will elevate your mind and allow you to walk into the Incredible You. You can find a copy on my website: www.incredibleoneenterprises.com.

I invite you to stop eating mental candy (television and radio) and focus on mental protein (books and empowerment CDs). When you start taking in more protein in your mental diet, you will notice an elevation that will take you to your next level. Expose yourself to the knowledge that will change your life by reading for just 30 minutes each day. Did you know that in doing so, you will achieve reading 50 books a year, which is the equivalent of receiving a PHD in your course of study in 2 years. Get excited and get reading, the Incredible You is waiting!

According to my favorite book, you are assured for success in life. So get excited, you are already everything you need to be to live Incredibly! So why do you let others talk you out of your destiny?

Never let your enemies (Incredible snatchers) tell you that you are worthless or insignificant. You have value in the eyes of God that is so great that it was worth dying for. Remember, you are a blessing to the world.

Darnyelle A. Jervey

Please don't become so spiritually minded that you think the enemy is just the devil, the enemy is your friend who every time you have a great idea, talks you down and convinces you that your idea is not a good one and you will never succeed. Unfortunately, we get caught up in the lies that people tell us about ourselves which allows us to become downtrodden, depressed and confused about who we are. Remember that childhood saying that sticks and stones may break your bones? Decide now that names or words will never hurt you.

When you share your dreams with people, not everyone will be able to embrace your heart's desires. Look at Joseph. He shared his dream with his brothers and they became extremely jealous. They were so jealous that they plotted to kill him. When God gives you a dream, others may get jealous and want to kill your dream. Those people may be your family and friends, but more than anything, they are Incredible snatchers. That is why the Incredible You must believe in yourself and your dreams, no matter what man says. And, more importantly, you must prevent them from stealing the Incredible out of you by developing the confidence and finding the tools that will make your dreams a reality.

Want to stop the Incredible snatchers? There must be a fire burning deep in your heart that never goes out especially because there will be others trying to extinguish the flames every chance they get.

Know from the beginning that your ideas won't make sense to everyone and it will take courage to persevere and work towards achieving your dreams. That is why you must be fully convinced that your dream will become a reality hook or crook.

There will be life situations that will happen to get in your way and attempt to take you off course from achieving

The Incredible You

your goal. It will be important at those times that you have and keep faith as a constant companion. When you know there's a dream in your heart, it was placed there to be completed. If you give up, you forfeit your destiny because my favorite book clearly tells you that He knows His plans to prosper you and give you hope and a future.

Giving up means that you don't want the future that God has promised you. I can see your future; let me tell you, it's Incredible!

Wisdom from my favorite book:
For I knows the plans I have for you, says the Lord. Plans to prosper you, to give you a hope and a future.

Unleash
Passion Abundance Confidence Expectation

Food for thought: Believe that your future is Incredible using the PACE Method.

Planning with Purposeful Passion:
How do you plan to overcome the Incredible snatchers in your life? What can you do today to stop giving up when you become discouraged or succumb to the lies that people say about you? What did you write in your journal today?

Achieving with an Attitude of Abundance:
What type of attitude do you have when you think about your future? Is there a need for any attitude adjustments to make sure that everything lines up with the abundance that you need to live your life Incredibly? What will you do to make the modification needed to carry out the Incredible You?

Creating with Consistent Confidence:
What steps have you taken to create an environment that fosters success as opposed to the negativity that currently surrounds you? What will confidence do to your personal outlook on life?

Executing with Enthusiastic Expectation:
At this point, the plan that you set in motion will enhance your outlook on life, what does your plan consistent of? What do you expect to change? Why?

Principle Six:

CREATE A LIFE WHERE EVERYTHING IS IN PROPER BALANCE AND PERSPECTIVE.

It is so important that you have balance in your life. I personally believe that God must be first, your family second and then everything else – if it makes you more comfortable to rank things after God and family, this would be the time to do it. But the bottom line is you need balance. I believe that when you do, as my favorite book says and seek God first, all things will be added to your life.

Too much of most things will eventually wear you out. Having a balance or priority scale, will help you to make sure that every area of your life is getting handled in proper perspective.

When you learn how to order your time, your most precious commodity, you will have learned to master another important facet of the Incredible You.

I think this is an extremely important principle. I always felt like I was a chicken with her head cut off. I think that when you are single, if you are not careful you will get so caught up in everything – work, church, friends, dating and staying busy, that you will not be able to relax. At least this was the case with me. I would leave my house at dark thirty and not return until dark thirty and when I came home, I was so tired that I could not even cook myself dinner or spend any quality time with my spirit. So I got burned out. In the early days of my career in Corporate

America, I was putting in "face time," which meant I was at work for twelve to fourteen hours a day. How can anyone be balanced with a life like that? Exactly. I didn't like myself or my life very much. I never went on dates and I felt so unfulfilled. But when I realized that there was more to life than my job, things really started to shift for me. You guessed it, my mindset changed and I decided to get some balance and perspective.

If you are a workaholic and spend more than your scheduled eight hours at your job, STOP. If you are active in church ministry but you can't even take time to cook a good dinner for your family, STOP. If you are constantly saying things like, "I don't ever have time for me," or "the last time I stopped to smell the roses was never," you need balance in your life. If you die tomorrow, the job and the ministry or whatever you are spending too much time doing, will go on without you. Get some balance; get a life of your own.

Create a proper balance and you will eliminate stress, strife and contention. I am a list person. Each day as I enter my office or each evening before I go to sleep, I make a "Most Important To Do" list for my company and my personal life. I strive for five tasks per list, each day. I chose five because I felt comfortable saying that I would actually get five things done every day. It also helps me to set an end to my day so that I can live that proper balance and enjoy everything that I like to have as a facet of my day, including television, God time, exercise, cooking dinner, etc. I believe in having a "daily win" in life. What I mean is that if you make it your goal to win everyday, your outlook on life and the daily tasks necessary to be who you are, will be easier to handle and duplicate.

Yes, I include my devotional time to make sure that I spend some time having 'a little talk with Jesus.' I make it my goal to have four fifteen-minute "praise breaks" so that I definitely get my time in with my Father. But do what works for you. This is just an example of how you can organize your day to make it the most effective and enjoy proper balance and perspective. Make sure that your day does include some form of devotional, prayer, meditation or other form of worship and quiet time with God to get centered and give you perspective. This will allow you to keep an attitude of gratitude and keep yourself grounded so that the trials of life and those uncontrollable items that spring up and knock us off our list don't bog us down and get us off track.

What I have found is that this simple exercise keeps me focused because I can't do everything on my plate each day. If only we could, right? But since that will never happen even if we worked 24 hours a day, 365 days a year, let's keep it real. The list helps you to "dump" your brain and then prioritize what has to get done.

Having one list for work and one for family ensures that all of the important tasks in each area of my life get handled. You may even need a third list, if you are active in ministry in your church, a Girl Scout leader, etc. Keeping lists will help you to set a daily win in your life. That way, as the sun sets on each day that you have been blessed to live, you can look back over that day and see what you have accomplished. When I learned this principle of leading and living from a list, my life shifted exponentially.

As women, we wear so many hats and often become discouraged when we cannot see the fruits of our labor. I don't want to leave the men out, as they too, I'm sure, experience frustrations when the day is over and there are more things to do. Let me encourage you, by having your "Most Important To Do" list, you will add order back into your life. You will find yourself with tangible results. And that will lead to more happiness as you complete more daily tasks each day without even thinking about it.

This exercise will also help you to get rid of those "I'm a slacker" or 'I can't do anything right" kind of comments because it will be right there documented for you. Another benefit of keeping a to do list is so that God may know our integrity, which is an important character trait for an Incredible person such as yourself!

You don't want to have so much going on that you can't enjoy the Incredible person that you are becoming, right? It's important that you do not spread yourself too thin because that can affect your integrity and focus. When you spread yourself too thin, you will get tired and frustrated and then you are not at your Incredible best and that's not the way that life should be. We all know that life is too short to not live the best life that we can.

Wisdom from my favorite book:
Let me be weighed in an even balance, that God may know mine integrity.

Unleash
Passion Abundance Confidence Expectation

Food for thought: Creating a life filled with proper balance and perspective using the PACE Method.

Planning with Purposeful Passion:
What kind of time manager are you? Do you see yourself making lists each day? If not, what will help you keep and maintain balance and perspective? Take the time right now to plan it.

Achieving with an Attitude of Abundance:
How will you make sure that you achieve balance and perspective with the right attitude? How will you feel when your chaotic life gets more order? How will you share your newly designed system with others so that they can enjoy the same abundance?

Creating with Consistent Confidence:
How long would it take you each day to create your "to-do" list with no more than five daily tasks at the start or end of your day? How will creating a daily win for yourself change your outlook on tasks? What will balance do to your confidence?

Executing with Enthusiastic Expectation:
How did you feel the first time that you completed your "Most Important Things To Do" list? Were you excited about the next day and an opportunity to do it all again? What has learning how to execute your priorities done for your level of expectation?

Principle Seven:

RELEASE YOURSELF FROM THE ISSUES, HURTS AND STRUGGLES OF YOUR PAST.

Many of you have read my memoir, *If You Understood My Past, You Would Understand My Praise*. My literary debut, which was my life's dream, is a book sharing and highlighting my story and identifying the issues of my past. My literary debut is a great example of releasing the past. As it is said, the past is a cancelled check, you can't get it back yet so many of us, keep allowing it to keep us from our future. Why?

I know that it may seem like a challenge, but we must all stop giving our past permission to speak. It is over, we must let it go. We are all afraid to unlock that little box that holds our family secrets and issues. All of us. For many years I pretended as if it didn't exist. But finally I wanted liberation. I was so sick and tired of using my past as an excuse. If I had a nickel for every time I said, "But because of how I was raised, I do things this way," I would be Oprah rich. The excuses, which are nothing more than the tools that incompetent people use to keep themselves bound to the issues that they are defending, got old. I realized that it was time to put on a pair of big girl panties and deal with my past.

After all, you cannot conquer what you refuse to confront. If you don't deal with it, it lingers and festers. It starts to stink and when you have an odor, everyone knows.

The Incredible You

And usually, no one tells you so you just walk around thinking you are cute yet smelling a hot mess! I don't have to tell you, that is not cute or productive.

Bondage is not going to get you closer to the Incredible You. You have to free yourself. I believe that if you conquer your past, you confirm your future. You've got some confirming to do!

We have all had things happen to us in the past. Big deal. It is over. You cannot change the past. It is no longer worth anything of substance. Why allow it to keep you from getting to where you want to be? There is no good reason why.

It happened years ago. Release it and trust that God will ease the pain in your heart. When you hold onto the issues of the past, you are the one who suffers. The one who wronged you is over it, if they are even aware that they hurt you at all. Let it go and walk into your future.

I love what my favorite book says, "If a man cleanses himself from the latter [the past], he will be an instrument for noble purposes, made holy, useful to the Master and prepared to do any good work." Need I say more?

When you get past what is behind you, you can be used for good things and be an example for others of what forward motion and thought can be. Writing my book, *If You Understood My Past, You Would Understand My Praise* was my way of helping others to realize that there is a praise on the other side of your past. Life gets better when you let things go. In fact, life becomes Incredible! Your mind is clear and void of confusion and your heart is whole, absent of anger, contempt or defeat. When your mind is clear and your heart is whole, Incredibleness is just around the corner and all you have to do is walk toward it.

When I think about the storms of my life, I get excited because they were all catalysts to my destiny! Had it not been for that betrayal, that abuse or that financial downfall, I would not be the Incredible person that I was born to be. I am able, by the grace of God, to be excited about the things that I have been through. They have made me stronger.

Think about Marvin Sapp's "Never Would Have Made It." He can only sing that song and you and I bob our heads and raise our hands in praise, if we let the past go. Think about it. If you are here, alive and healthy, you ought to be praising right now. You have already proven that you can make it through other life trials. So get excited that you will come out of the past stronger, wiser and better. Let it go.

I have decided to P.R.E.S.S. or to Persistently Run Expecting Supernatural Success. A woman in my church, Sheila, shared her testimony with us and said that she realized that in order to make it through, she had to P.R.E.S.S. and she created this amazing acronym. Sheila is amazing and through this acronym, she will bless so many lives. She has already blessed mine.

2008 was a year of transition for me. There were many issues, obstacles and constraints that I had to P.R.E.S.S. through. I can still shake my head in realization of what this year of new beginnings has been to me. There were lots of new beginnings, just not the warm and fuzzy ones that everyone was expecting at the dawning of the New Year. But as I stand on the verge of 2009, I am stronger, wiser and better because of all the obstacles I overcame in 2008. I decided to P.R.E.S.S. before I met Sheila and learned of her Incredible acronym.

But now that I know it and her, I am even more Incredible! Thanks Sheila Mathis; I appreciate you and your willingness to share this amazing concept with me. Because of her acronym, Incredible lives are changing.

The Incredible You

Pressing is moving forward regardless of what is coming your way. It is important that you move ahead persistently. It means that you have decided that you will not give up. You will keep going no matter what comes your way. Running is about action versus standing still and letting things happen to you. Running allows you to be proactive to change and stress. Standing still is the sign of completed work; where as running is about the realization that the work is not yet done. Decide that you will embrace the change and embrace it with a supernatural expectation.

Wow, if you are not empowered now, I don't know what to tell you. Success will be yours when you decide to take action against the problems, trials and tribulations that come your way. You must P.R.E.S.S. You must decide that the past is just that and your future is so bright that you need shades to handle all of what is coming your way. The Incredible You is just over the horizon from your past hurts, failures and strife. Don't you want to meet the Incredible You? You better P.R.E.S.S.

Wisdom from my favorite book:
Brethren, I do not count myself to have apprehended; but one thing I do, forgetting those things which are behind and reaching forward to those things which are ahead, I press toward the goal for the prize of the upward call of God in Christ Jesus.

Unleash
Passion Abundance Confidence Expectation

Food for thought: Releasing the past using the PACE Method.

Planning with Purposeful Passion:
Admittedly, letting go of the past can be difficult. What can you plan to do to help ease the difficulty of this task? Do you honestly believe that your passion is linked to your ability to P.R.E.S.S.? Why or Why not?

Achieving with an Attitude of Abundance:
As you conquer the issues of the past, your attitude and abundance levels will increase. What will an abundant attitude do for your ability to achieve your life's dreams? What did you write in your journal today?

Creating with Consistent Confidence:
Confidence can be hindered by the past. What are you already implementing in your life that will allow your confidence to increase despite the thought of those things which are behind you?

Executing with Enthusiastic Expectation:
Expect release and release will come. What does this statement mean to you?

Principle Eight:

*E*XPECT UNMERITED FAVOR IN YOUR LIFE.

It's been said that "favor ain't fair." I must admit, I know that's right! What is favor, you ask. Favor is preferential treatment and shift in the universe that means that everything you want you get. Are you rejoicing already? When you walk uprightly and focus on living a positive life, there is not one thing that will be withheld from you.

One of my favorite sayings is "Expect Incredible things and Incredible things will happen." If you want unmerited favor, you must expect it. Is it really that simple? It depends on who you are and your outlook on life. Regardless, you are half way there when you expect Incredible things to happen.

Expectation is derived from purpose. When you know your purpose, what you are here to do, you will expect to establish it and work toward and in it. Enthusiastic expectation is essential if you want to become the Incredible You.

Remember that what you speak you bring about; so you must speak with enthusiastic expectation. When you expect anything to happen, you usually speak about it. Let's say you applied for a job and you just know that the job is yours. Don't you tell people that you are getting a new job? Exactly, when you do that, you are living this principle to the Incredible You. Life and death lies in the power of your tongue and when you speak life, you will experience living. I am not talking about existing, no, I am talking about living: Living your destiny, dreams and passion. Not just living them any ol' way, but living them with enthusiastic expectation. If you want unmerited favor, you must speak favor over your life.

Let's journey back to another principle in the process of becoming the Incredible You: Never give up no matter what others say about you. If you recall, when you have made a non-negotiable decision to persevere no matter who says don't, you will be able to set an expectation for greatness in your life.

Your mind can be a battleground if you don't protect it and expect that Incredible things are happening in your life. You must speak what you expect to receive.

Enthusiastic expectation means that you are excited about what is going to happen. Your glass is half-full and you know that you know that you know that something great is in the works for you. I know firsthand that it can be difficult to walk around with a glass that is half-full when everything around you is empty. Take this economy; for example, I know that this economy is enough to drive you to destruction. But when you expect unmerited favor, it may not make sense to the world but you will know that you will not lack even during these perilous times. You have an expectation that is Incredible. Things are happening despite what others have to say and that is precisely the key to unleashing the Incredible You.

When you expect favor, does that mean that you will never struggle or experience pressure? Does it mean that everyday at your house will be sunny and shiny? Of course not. But the difference between the Incredible You and the average Joe is that you expect that things will get better. My favorite book promises that joy comes in the morning. You know that all you have to do is wake up and things will be better. You will not succumb to the pressures of

The Incredible You

what just happened. Instead, you will get excited because what the Incredible snatchers mean for bad, God is already turning around for your good.

One of the most important principles I ever learned says this: ask and believe that you will receive it. After you ask and believe, begin to act as if it is already done, and that is expectation. Expectation means that there is nothing stopping the flow that is already on its way to you. Think of a train; once its course is set, it keeps moving until it arrives at its destination. There is nothing that can stop a train that is already in motion. Your ability to expect Incredible things in your life must replicate this thought process. By deciding that you will act as if it already is, you are giving wings to your desires and you will be able to watch them take flight.

When the joy of the Lord is your strength, even when you struggle, you will be able to expect that you are coming out of it on top. It's like Diana Ross sang in her song "I'm Coming Out," you will want to make sure that the world knows because you expect to have a new attitude and a new way of looking at that glass on the table. Get excited because you will know that you are the head and not the tail, you are above and not beneath. You are entitled to walk uprightly and that makes you Incredible!

Wisdom from my favorite book:
The Lord will give grace and glory; No good thing will He withhold from those who walk uprightly.

Unleash
Passion Abundance Confidence Expectation

Food for thought: Expecting unmerited favor using the PACE Method.

Planning with Purposeful Passion:
Do you expect favor in your life? Why or Why Not? What do you plan to do to begin to enjoy the benefits of expecting favor? How will favor enhance your passion?

Achieving with an Attitude of Abundance:
Is your expectation of favor linked directly to abundance? Why or Why not? How will your attitude change when you start to expect unmerited favor in your life?

Creating with Consistent Confidence:
Consistency is the key to confidence. What are you going to put into motion in your life to turn off the highs and lows that can have a tendency to cause your confidence levels to wane?

Executing with Enthusiastic Expectation:
What is your definition of enthusiasm? What will enthusiasm do to your ability to expect unmerited favor in your life? What will you change to make this principle a staple in your life?

Principle Nine:

*D*ECIDE TODAY THAT VISION IS YOUR KEY TO VICTORY.

When you have vision, you have victory. My favorite book says that without vision, people perish. So ask yourself, what happens when you have vision? You live an Incredible life!

Can you see the invisible? Do you have the foresight to determine what the end is going to be in your life? Do you expect to win? Can you see those things that do not exist and know in your heart that they will come to pass, no matter what it looks like right at this minute?

Beginning with the end in mind is pivotal to becoming the Incredible You.

I want more than anything for you to be a visionary. Visionaries are able to see beyond what is right in front of them; they are able to think outside of the box. Visionaries know that their best ideas are found on the road less traveled. One of my favorite original quote is "look behind, get stuck; look in front of you maintain; but look ahead and grow."

Visionaries are willing to have disappointments along the way to victory. We all make mistakes; but, visionaries take those mistakes and learn from them to set them up for success. I love the phrase "a set back is a set up for a come back." Visionaries live this phrase consistently in their lives. They don't get caught up in the current situation, they are always thinking ahead to the next opportunity to see their vision in action. Vision is a mindset, which says that you can do anything because of the belief that rests in your bosom and is powered by your mind.

I love what Robert Collier had to say about vision, "It reaches beyond the thing that is, into the conception of what can be. Imagination gives you the picture. Vision gives you the impulse to make the picture your own."

Visionaries refuse to compromise their integrity on the way to victory. Visionaries refuse to take no for an answer. As they watch their vision take shape, they become excited and enthusiastic. The thought of victory excites the visionary. They have decided that vision is their key to victory. Visionaries are extremely optimistic people; they see lemons and grab the sugar so that they can start mixing up the lemonade.

Become a big thinker and you will experience Incredible results in your life. I personally believe that it should be your goal to dream so big that only God can make it happen. I mean so big that people think you are crazy when you share your dreams with them; those are the kinds of dreams that visionaries have. Vision is what allows new dreams and ideas to consistently be born into your spirit.

When I think of vision, I am taken back to my personal journey in Mary Kay Cosmetics. I became a consultant because I learned to love the product and I had no desire to pay full price for those products that I loved. After considering the business opportunity, my vision was just to get my own products and to keep the product line to myself. However, that vision was changed one day at work. A young lady came into my office and asked me for a catalog. When she returned two hours later, she had over $600 worth of orders from other women in the office. My mindset prior to that occurrence had been limited. I thought that as a black woman, no one would want those products, even though I loved them personally. Because my mind was boxed in, I was unable to see the invisible. With that one action, my mind shifted and I realized that this business could prove to be a viable solution to the financial strain I was experiencing at that time in my life.

I began to visualize myself debt free. No matter what my checkbook or credit card statements said, I believed that the victory would be mine. So I became an active beauty consultant and I started to share the product with consistency. In one year, I was able to eliminate over $15,000 worth of credit card debt. What changed? My vision.

From there, I continued to believe that my vision was the key to the victory in my life. I decided that I wanted more and the Mary Kay opportunity would help me to get it. Everything I wanted was not material, but I wanted flexibility and I wanted to do something positive. My vision, once again, shifted and I began to see the invisible in a big way. It became my goal to win a Pink Cadillac. Now, I know that you're thinking that every woman who joins Mary Kay wants to win a Pink Cadillac. And, you are probably correct. But I was different. I had the vision and the foresight to actually make it happen.

Excitedly, I shared my vision and dream with those who were close to me and they attempted to bring me back down to reality. They told me that I was crazy and no one really got a pink car. They tried to deflate my bubble, but I was clear. My vision was focused and most importantly, I believed in my ability to make it happen. I have always been ambitious and I have always believed that I was destined for greatness and so I did what I knew to do, I went for it. My first step was to create my plan. Visionaries plan.

Darnyelle A. Jervey

After I set up my plan, which included realistic timeframes and lots of research, I went to work. In order to get a Pink Cadillac, I needed to be a Sales Director. So I became one. It took me fourth months to complete that goal. What is notable is that when I decided I wanted to be a Sales Director, I had two of the eight team members needed to begin the process. In one month, I recruited ten women, giving me twelve total team members going into the qualification process. Visionaries exceed their goals without any issue because of their foresight.

Once I became a Sales Director, my next plan was to become a consistent performer in assisting my unit to achieve their goals. I became a Sales Director in July of 2003 and I became a Cadillac Director in September 2005. How did I do it? I ensured that my vision was never influenced by things or people around me. Sure, there were Incredible snatchers along the way. Some were in my family, some were my so-called friends and even other Mary Kay consultants doubted my ability to achieve my vision. But I decided that my vision was the key to victory. My victory was to break another belief barrier in my community. At that time, my National Area had never experienced a black woman achieving that level of success. Because I was able to see the invisible, I knew that with God's help, I could do the impossible, which was to become the first black woman in my National Area and the second in the state of Delaware to earn and drive the prestigious "trophy on wheels" at that time.

Sometimes as a visionary you may not have the direct path to your dreams but you must be willing to go through the maze of life and find your way to your purpose and passion. Once there, as a visionary you will find a way to link your steps to your destiny because your foresight in all situations will show you that you are victorious.

The Incredible You

I never doubted that I could have a Pink Cadillac. In actuality, during my Mary Kay tenure, I enjoyed five career cars and two of them were the Pink Cadillac. As a visionary, I knew that if I devoted quality time, attention, and affection towards my dream and others who were helping me to achieve my dream, we would all be victors. Why is that important? It's important because I am not the only person who can decide they want something and develop a plan to make it happen, if you so endeavor, you can do the same.

May I suggest you start by creating a vision board which encapsulates everything that you want from the universe? Now, the key to your vision board is that it is specific and it is based solely on your vision. Please do not mistake this: a vision board will not make you happy; you cannot believe that in receiving these things you will become Incredible. No, you must realize that the Incredible is already tucked on the inside of you. Your vision board is a vehicle by which it becomes unleashed. As it is said and I have shared before, what gets attended to gets done. So by creating a board that highlights everything in detail that you want in your life, you help to ensure that you receive it. Again, you are realizing that vision is your key to victory. When I say be specific, I mean it. Down to the penny, how much money do you want in your back account? What does the exact house where you want to raise your children look like – inside and out? That goes on your board in explicit detail.

Creating a mental picture and taking a snapshot of what you want to enjoy in your life is pivotal to this principle. You must be able to see it; you will never be it if you don't see it first.

Visionaries refuse to allow what they see to hinder what they believe. They know that manifestation is a process.

Visionaries know that things are not always what they seem. Even when the situation is not a positive one, visionaries get excited about how to turn the situation around and keep themselves on pace to achieve their overall goal. Vision is about looking at your checkbook and not seeing the money you need to pay your bills, but being optimistic and realizing that when you work in faith, all of your needs will be met. Visionaries don't look at what is they look at what is to come.

Vision is the key to maximizing and unlocking your potential. Decide today that vision is the key to your victory and you will live and be on the way to achieving your biggest goals and dreams. Not a visionary? Make a non-negotiable decision that the time is now to receive the victory in your life. You can be a visionary as soon as you realize that all that it takes is for you to be able to say right now that you are able to accomplish that which you desire. If you can see it, it can be a reality. Do you have faith? Do you believe that you can do anything to which you put your mind? If you are able to answer yes, it is time to decide what your vision looks like. In this time of economic downturn, vision is not being concerned about your current status but looking toward the hills...

Although you can't see it now, you have full knowledge and belief that you possess what it takes to move from victim to visionary. If you want to have victory, you have to be optimistic. Is your glass half-full? When your glass is half-full, you are closing in on your victory. When you are able to see clearly those things which do not yet exist, you are walking in a liberating victory because those dreams, goals and desires are just an action away from becoming reality and catapulting you into a personal triumph.

As a success coach and empowerment speaker, I am often challenged to help people develop vision that sees the

The Incredible You

invisible and believes that anything is possible. When I think of vision, I am reminded of a child who has an imaginary friend. With their imaginary friend in tow, that child pursues situations and obstacles with a consistent confidence and enthusiastic expectation that is unparalleled in the world today. I often wonder why our minds don't allow us to think and act as children when it comes to taking the necessary risks and faith walks to live an Incredible life filled with dream fulfillment and passion, abundance, confidence and expectation. Wasn't everything much simpler when you were a child?

As adults, we don't believe in imaginary friends, but when you have vision, you see possibilities and results that are not visible to others. Being a visionary is an important key to becoming the Incredible You.

Situations are changed because of vision. Nothing great in this life was ever accomplished without vision. Think of anyone that you admire in this world. No matter who he/she is and how significant his/her triumph, he/she possessed an uncanny ability to see the invisible and do the impossible; otherwise, you would not look up to him/her.

Need an example of what vision can do for you? Take Colonel Sanders of the infamous KFC chain. When he retired, he received his first social security check of less than $100, he was disappointed but he had something worth much more....his recipe for finger licking good chicken. He went out on sales calls to many restaurants offering to make chicken in their kitchens for only a portion of the proceeds of the chicken sales and they laughed at him! But his vision kept him going. He did not give up after that 1st, 2nd or 100th "no."

How many of us would have stopped?

But because of his vision, he knew that something more was around the corner and he decided to P.R.E.S.S.

forward. Did you know that he received 1,008 "no's" before he got a "yes?!" And the rest is history. My point? Vision keeps you going long after others have given up on you. Vision says no matter what, I believe in myself and because of that, I am worth more than what man has to say about me, my goal, my dream or my idea.

When you have the foresight to see those things that do not exist currently but know in your heart, mind and spirit that they will come to pass, you are becoming a visionary, much like the people you admire. No vision is too small and I admonish you not to compare your triumphs with those of others as we are all on an individual journey.

As I have said before, visionaries think outside of the box. Visionaries are able to do things a little differently to get a victorious result. Visionaries never give up because they don't know what is coming around the next corner. It is always too early to throw in the towel on your hopes, dreams and desires. I like to say that visionaries wobble but they don't fall down because they are fully convinced that what they see will come to pass.

What are you defining with your goals, dreams and desires? If you are not sure, then may I suggest that you consult your Maker? He is, after all, the Maker of you and He defined the purpose of you.

You must decide now that vision is your key to victory and walk it out. My favorite books says that without vision you will die. I agree; if you can't see where you are going, you will get so lost along the way that you will be overtaken by fear, angst, doubt and despair and they all lead to death. God will always give you more on your way than He ever will when you are standing still. It's almost like a GPS: the GPS only gives you one direction at a time because it knows that you cannot handle knowing every step in the journey at one time. But in order to take a journey, you have to start somewhere, why not start with your vision? Having vision is pivotal if you want to live and achieve anything. So think, see and then do. You can do it, Incredible One. I believe in you. The Incredible You is waiting; he or she is standing just behind your vision.

Wisdom from my favorite book:
Where there is no vision, the people perish: but blessed is he who keeps the law.

Unleash
Passion Abundance Confidence Expectation

Food for thought: Decide that vision is the key to your victory with the PACE Method.

Planning with Purposeful Passion:
What is your dream? Can you see it happening? What is your plan to watch your vision come into view? Write it down. Create your vision board with the specific things you want to see manifested in your life.

Achieving with an Attitude of Abundance:
Knowing is half of the battle. Realizing what you have just written about your vision, what is the next step? Is your mind prepared for the journey your vision will take it on? How's your attitude? What about your abundance level? Explain.

Creating with Consistent Confidence:
Creativity is an important component of vision. Confidence helps to take the vision to the next level. Write down what you plan to do to illustrate the consistency in your confidence as it relates to your vision.

Executing with Enthusiastic Expectation:
Once a vision has been identified, enthusiasm typically arrives next. But, what do you expect? Deep down where no one else can see, do you really believe that your vision will become a reality? What are you prepared to do to make sure that it happens just as you expect?

Principle Ten:

*I*NCREASE YOUR SELF-IMAGE; YOU ARE WHO YOU SAY YOU ARE.

When you look in the mirror, who looks back at you? Do you like what you see? Are you overly critical about who you are? Do you only see the physical you or do you look deeper and analyze the real you, the you that no one sees unless you decide to become transparent?

These may be tough questions to answer, but understanding who you are is another key component to becoming the Incredible You.

I love that song by Lupe Fiasco...you are who you say you are, a superstar, have no fear....

As a young girl, I definitely struggled with my self-image. I would see any girl and instantly want to be her because I always assumed that she must have a better existence than me. I remember this one girl in grade school in particular. She was pretty with light skin and long wavy hair. Her clothes were always neat and fit her so perfectly. She had perfect teeth and her parents were like the Huxtables, one was a lawyer and the other a doctor. In my mind, she had it all. I was just a squirrel trying to get a nut; but she held the bag.

As a result, my self-image was very distorted, I hated myself. I could never do anything right. I never dressed right, my hair never looked right. I could never talk in front of the class with poise and ease. I always took longer to complete class assignments. In my eyes, I was a failure.

When I looked in the mirror, I was convinced that other people did not see what I saw in that same mirror. All I could see were my failures and shortcomings. The lenses that I looked at life through were dismal and gray. I did not believe that I was pretty; yet I heard it consistently. I thought people were just making fun of me. I thought that I was ugly and convinced myself that no one would ever want to love and be around me. I lived in the shadow of my horrible self-image for a long time and I missed out on so much because I was who I thought I was. I walked around in fear with my head down because I felt that I was not significant.

That was very damaging to my life. Today, I am grateful that the cloud of doubt that surrounded me has been lifted so that I could see myself clearly. Today I can see myself as I was created to live: in abundance.

God's Word tells me that I am the apple of His eye. Once I let Him into my heart and got to know Him for myself, I started to realize that He already loved me like I desired to be loved. With that realization, I could pick up my shattered existence and cement my self-esteem together.

Today, my self-esteem and my self-image are on point; they are sugar sharp! I am so excited about the woman that God made me that I created an affirmation or power statement to share who I am with others every chance I get:

> "Driven, determined, striving for the best; A woman on the move, a sister of success; Focused on the future, a diva supreme; The secret place where dreamers go to dream; Favored by God to empower people's lives; Simply by allowing Christ to be my guide; As I dream so big that only He can make it happen; Keeping Him first is my

The Incredible You

most valuable weapon; Stepping out on faith, dressed to a tee; Attracting big thinkers with abundance mentality; Expanding my vision beyond what eyes can see; Mediocrity has been removed from my vocabulary; I stand before you and I am destined to excel; I am powerful, I am poised and my name is Darnyelle."

What is my point? God made me exactly who I am and more importantly because I believe what He says about me, I can get excited about the woman looking back at me in the mirror. Because He is no respecter of persons, He has already done the same for you. God made you exactly the way that you are supposed to be. Once I realized that, the sky was the limit and I could increase my self-image and embrace the woman that I was born to be.

You already possess every component necessary to be who God wants you to be. Who are you?

So often we get caught up in what society says about us. But why does society get to label and determine who you are? Why would you give people who mean nothing to you the satisfaction of defining you? You may be thinking, "Yeah, you're right," but we do it every day. I suggest that you give God the satisfaction of defining you, as He has already done repeatedly in His Word.

Don't try to be who others think you should be; be authentic. Be original. You are the only you for a reason; even if you have a twin, you came down the birth canal alone and you have your own unique set of finger prints for a reason. Be you. You are a work of art; be a masterpiece. Be yourself. God thinks you are Incredible.

Here are a few things that God's Word says you are:
- You are able.   Phil 4:13
- You are beautiful.   Psalm 149:4
- You are bold.   Proverbs 28:1

- You are chosen. — I Peter 2:9
- You are confident. — I John 4:17
- You are filled with joy. — John 17:13
- You are gifted. — Romans 12:6
- You are His handiwork. — Eph 2:10
- You have a life of abundance. — John 10:10
- You are loved. — John 3:16
- You are on the winning side. — Col 2:15

God didn't have time to make a nobody, only a somebody. You are somebody who is extremely important to God. You don't have to be taller, thinner, shorter, fatter or cuter to be who you were created to be. You are already exactly who you need to be. It is not necessary that you gain weight or lose weight, grow taller or shrink, become beautiful or less appealing. You are complete.

When God made you, He was just showing off. Being who you were created to be and increasing your self-image is important to God. When we are born, we are given a name, which begins to shape our identity. We each have our own unique set of fingerprints that makes us like no one else in the world for a reason. You must get comfortable in your own skin.

You were created on purpose; you were not an accident. Additionally, God did not create you to be like anyone else. You are the one and only you for a reason. To increase your self-image, believe in yourself. You must make a choice and decide that you will believe in who you are and that you will embrace who you were created to be. Remember that attitude is 95% of who you are, so it is important to decide now that you will believe in yourself and you will increase your self-image by reflecting on who you are. I encourage you to take an introspective look at yourself and change those things in you that do not line up with the divine plan for you and your life.

The Incredible You

To increase yourself image, you need to change what you say about yourself. You must begin to speak life and success to yourself. I can assure you that you will even have to encourage yourself from time to time but in order for you to be able to successfully do that, you must believe in yourself. It does not matter what other people think about you, your self-image is based on what you think about yourself. It is so true what they say, "Whether you think you can or you can't, you're right." No one will ever be able to talk you out of what you believe to be true about yourself. So if you want to be better, do better and see better, you must first believe better.

If you could see yourself like I see you, you'd see that you are Incredible.

Wisdom from my favorite book:
For as a man thinks, so is he.

Unleash
Passion Abundance Confidence Expectation

Food for thought: Increase your self image with the PACE Method.

Planning with Purposeful Passion:
Write your own power statement. Who are you? Do you know? Now is the time to let the world know. If you are still unsure, return to this place when you are comfortable writing your power statement.

Achieving with an Attitude of Abundance:
How do you feel about yourself? What is your attitude when you look at yourself in the mirror? Write how you are feeling right now in your journal.

Creating with Consistent Confidence:
Confidence is an important component of the Incredible You. What steps can you take to consistently create opportunities to increase your confidence in your self-image?

Executing with Enthusiastic Expectation:
When you expect Incredible things, Incredible things will happen. Outline your expectation plan for what your increased self-image will mean to the Incredible You.

Principle Eleven:

*B*E HAPPY

I love Mary J. Blige's song "Be Happy." It is truly all that I believe that you want. Wouldn't it be great to find the life that is yours? Even when I think of Bobby Darrin and his hit "Don't Worry, Be Happy," I have to smile. The time for drama, depression, desperation and drought is over! The time has come for passion, abundance, confidence and expectation. It's time to be happy.

Happiness is a state of mind that is so essential to the Incredible You. I think so many people have it wrong; they think that things make them happy. What I know to be true is that being happy is not an end result of getting lots of things. Being happy is the place to start if you want to become the Incredible You. Think about it - when you feel good everything seems to go your way. You may call it being lucky or having a good day. I call it being happy and ultimately fulfilled. When in actuality, the way you feel is the reason for the success you are enjoying at that moment; your mind has allowed you to experience a feeling of euphoria.

It may take you a minute to realize that the success you feel is as a result of your state of mind. But once you do, you will want to strive to always be in your happy place. Happiness, when mastered, will prevent days when you are unhappy. Your outlook on life will be different and you will be able to consistently see the joy in every situation.

When I learned to be happy, so many things in my life changed. You've heard the old adage "When life gives you lemons make lemonade?" Well, I took that phrase to heart and started to find a way to make lemonade out of every situation in my life. We choose to allow ourselves to be victims or victors and happiness is a choice. Becoming the Incredible You is a choice. Clearly it is your goal or you would not be reading this book – smile.

Life is full of choices and choosing to be happy is a very good one. Not only do life and death lie in the power of the tongue, but they also lie in the power of the mind. When you choose to be happy, you are choosing a lifetime of happiness and fulfillment that is out of this world.

Want to turn a sad day into a happy one? Pay attention to your thoughts. Like the Bible says, "As a man thinks, so is he." So if you want to be happy, you must think happiness. I believe that so many of us have an invalid definition of happiness so to be sure, I would like to define it for you.

According to Webster's New World Dictionary, happiness is having, showing or causing a feeling of great pleasure, contentment or joy; favored by circumstance. I want you to get excited because happiness means that you are favored. As discussed in an earlier principle, expecting unmerited favor in your life is an important part of the Incredible You. I encourage you to expect unmerited happiness and allow the way that you look at the world to shadow all of the experiences that you have while you are here. I mean, come on, since you've got to be here anyway until you're not, you might as well love life.

Take it from me; I have been a person with a bad attitude. There is nothing enlightened about having a negative outlook on life. In fact, I remember always being miserable and always blaming someone else for my struggles when truly the culprit was me. Because my view of life was distorted and I was operating from a place of anger, I missed a lot.

I decided to change my destiny by changing my mindset; I decided to be happy. Simply put, I started to look for the "silver lining" in all situations and before I knew it, my glass was half-full and I was optimistic as opposed to the pessimist that I use to be. Every time I noticed myself in a good mood, I captured that moment and stored it in my heart. After a while, I had a bank of good thoughts and feelings to go back to and draw from when I was not having a pleasant experience.

Realize you are in charge of your well being and control it with your thoughts and emotions. So be happy first. Go for it. You deserve the best!

Bottom line: You must believe in the power to be happy. There is nothing more powerful in this life than the power of belief. When you can believe that anything is possible, the Incredible You will be front and center. I love the story of the bumblebee, who according to aerodynamic principles should not be able to fly. But the bumblebee believed in his heart that in order to serve his life function, he was going to have to get around and he did it; he flew away breaking a significant belief barrier.

As a child, I believed that I was supposed to be more than what I was experiencing. That belief in my heart, although it laid dormant for years, was always there inspiring me to be better, stronger and wiser. I believe that nothing happens by mistake and so I had to experience a life of non-belief so that when I started to believe, the power of my own belief and faith would be magnified for myself and others. When I started to believe in myself and believe that my dreams were possible and not just figments of my imagination, my life really started. I got a new attitude and in so doing put myself in a position to influence my future.

Darnyelle A. Jervey

I have consistently said that life is 95% attitude and we get to make a choice every day about how we want that day to go. I decide everyday to live with a full glass and an outlook on life that tells me that I can do anything because I believe that I can. I choose to be happy.

Belief is the most passionate gift in life; it is an illustration in our ability to trust. When what we believe is true and what we believe is possible, it will become a truth and possibility for us. I encourage you again to be happy, the Incredible You deserves it!

Wisdom from my favorite book:
For we are His workmanship, created in Christ Jesus for good works, which God prepared beforehand that we should walk in them.

Unleash
Passion Abundance Confidence Expectation
Food for thought: Be Happy using the PACE Method.

Planning with Purposeful Passion:
What can you plan to do differently to become happy on purpose? What about who you are makes you happy? What makes you sad? Write your thoughts in your journal.

Achieving with an Attitude of Abundance:
List some of the reasons you have to be happy. Place a star by the ones that have to do with your attitude. No stars? Start by writing down what about your life's disposition you will adjust to find some happiness despite what may be going wrong around you.

Creating with Consistent Confidence:
It has been said that we create our opportunities for happiness. Do you believe this statement? Why or Why Not? What can you do to create happiness in your life starting today?

Executing with Enthusiastic Expectation:
Do you expect to be happy? Do you just meander through life trying to do just enough to get by? Do you want to change your expectation quotient? How can you execute the needed change? What does happiness mean to you?

Principle Twelve:

*L*IVE TO LOVE.

"*I* love you!" Those are three words that every person waits with baited breath to hear. Whether the declaration is made platonically, romantically or even amongst family, we wait for others to affirm our place in this world by telling us that we matter, that we are loved. But a more powerful declaration that we should all say early and often in our lives is "I love me! And God loves me!"

We put far too much emphasis on how others feel about us. We need to focus on loving ourselves first in order to become Incredible. Once you love yourself, you can freely share that powerful emotion with others in the form of relational love, brotherly or sisterly love, and even servant love. The key to living to love extends your boarders and helps you to look at life through Incredible eyes!

Love is patient, love is kind, love is humble, love is caring, live is pure, love is filled with hope, love is faithful and true, love is forgiving, love is selfless and serving, love is wise, love understands, love never ends and most importantly, love is God.

I believe that the greatest accomplishment of any person is to love themselves and others. An important part of life is learning to love. The Bible says it best. "Love bears all things, believes all things, hopes all things, endures all things and never fails." When you love yourself because God first loved you, you will never fail. And trust me, that is where you want to be.

The Incredible You

I believe wholeheartedly that self-love is the catalyst for dreams realized. When you love yourself, you will naturally love everything that goes along with who you are – your dreams, goals, ideas, etc. I think we first learn how to love ourselves from our parents; how they interact one with another and how they treat us. In my case, my parents were not good love role models and unfortunately many of us suffer from the same type of upbringing. Although we may not learn it from home, we can seek out relationships with friends and family that can give us that love quotient and help us to define ourselves.

Because of my home life, I always sought out friends who had an amazing family, the kind I always wanted. They ate dinner together, they took trips, they talked and even when they were getting on each other's nerves, there was an unspoken yet powerful emotion that resided with them and kept them together. Love is beautiful and I am thankful for my friends that showed me early and often what true love means; and how when it exists in purity, it can spur the most amazing dreams in its recipients.

My goal for you is that you learn the true definition of love. I think that far too many people use the word without truly understanding its meaning and the ramifications of it. Love, when used incorrectly can be a destructive force; it can prevent lives from continuing to be lived, it can kill and harm innocent people. But love was created out of the goodness of God. You are becoming Incredible; it is absolutely essential that you learn how to live to love.

Before you can offer love to someone else, you must love yourself. When you love yourself, the realization that you are worth more, the fact that you are already Incredible will be readily apparent to everyone around you. Self-love will help you to walk taller, speak clearer, display strength and prevent others from being able to impact who you are.

If you are secure, you will be happy. The joy in your heart will be unparallel to any other experience in life.

What's even more important is that when your circle of influence includes other people who love themselves, they will not be uneasy or jealous of the confidence and love that you have in who you are. If others are not embracing the love and confidence that you exude, that may be a clue that they should not be people that you spend significant time with as they may turn into Incredible snatchers and suck the love right out of you.

Love is a powerful thing; it was created for you to celebrate it as often as possible and to be able to illustrate it everyday in your life. Love allows renewal, enrichment and fulfillment. Loving yourself offers you as well as others who know you and spend time in your space the gift of acceptance, forgiveness and faith. Love is Incredible.

Love creates hope and hope creates dreams and dreams will become a reality when exercised with passion and consistency. Love believes in the sun even when it's raining. Love believes the best in every situation.

When you love yourself, you will be able to demand love from others in the form of honesty, integrity and respect in relationships – business or personal. Won't it feel good to operate in self-love? As you live to love, start with yourself, then your fellow man and watch the soul of the Incredible You prosper.

Wisdom from my favorite book:
For God so loved the world that He sent His only begotten son that whosoever should believe on Him, shall not die but have life everlasting.

Unleash
Passion Abundance Confidence Expectation
Food for thought: Living to love using the PACE Method.

Planning with Purposeful Passion:
Write yourself a love letter. Be sure to include why you love yourself and what you are most proud of about you. Seal it and mail it to yourself. Then when you need to be reminded on how to live to love, read and reread it and become purposeful about the importance of self-love in your life.

Achieving with an Attitude of Abundance:
What is your attitude toward love? How important is it that other people demonstrate and articulate their love for you? Be honest with yourself.

Creating with Consistent Confidence:
How do you illustrate your love for other people? Do the people in your life know that you love them? Are you consistent with your form of expression? Are you confident that others know how you feel about yourself – this should be based on how you carry and talk about who you are? Remember, you are who you say you are.

Executing with Enthusiastic Expectation:
If you haven't started it already, be sure to start your love letter. Executing your feelings for yourself in writing gives them validity and will help you to assess what you believe your self-worth is. People will never treat you better than you treat yourself as you are unconsciously giving them permission to treat you that way. What will change? How will you make sure that it happens?

Principle Thirteen:

*E*XECUTE YOUR GOALS AND DREAMS WITH ENTHUSIASTIC EXPECTATION.

Enthusiasm simply means God within. The Incredible You must ensure that the God within you is consistently radiating so that others can see His Incredibleness in and around you. Expectation means to believe with all of your heart that the thing that you are wishing and hoping for and even planning for will come your way. As I said a few principles ago, I believe that we must expect Incredible things so that Incredible things happen in our lives. Through this, the God within us that radiates from us based on our level of enthusiasm. His radiation in turn will propel others as well as ourselves to have a level of expectation that is supernatural. Our enthusiastic expectation will help us to execute because of the confidence that we have in ourselves. You cannot hit a ball out of the park if you don't try to hit the ball. When you expect enthusiastically, you will execute Incredibly.

What is the point of setting goals and dreams if you have no intention of following through with the execution of them? More importantly, if you are not expecting to achieve those goals, why would you even take the time to set them? I think you've got my point. A logical step to becoming the Incredible You is to expect that all this work and preparation for the last twelve principles will not be in vain. I hope that you expect at the end of this intensive process to be Incredible. Right? Of course you do! Well, at this step in the process, here is what is important. The keys to being a success and executing all that you are learning about who you are and who you will become.

Let's journey back to my example of my tenure in Mary Kay Cosmetics. I was clear, my goal was set and it was non-negotiable that I would win a Pink Cadillac. It was up to me after setting that goal to execute it with enthusiastic expectation. I expected to win one because I had planned and determined my strategy and course of action. I was enthusiastic about it. I shared my goal with everyone. I did this because I was clear and I was confident in my abilities. **I do not encourage you to run around town broadcasting your dream if your faith and conviction are not set on the end result. Let me be clear. If you are not fully convinced in your own mind that the dream will be achieved, I suggest that you keep it to yourself.** Remember that everywhere you go, you have the propensity to run into Incredible snatchers and they will grab a hold of your goal and observe your lack of confidence and pounce on you. Through prayer, they will begin to speak against your goals. Remember, life and death does lie in the power of the tongue. Incredible snatchers have as much power as you do if you are not fully convinced in your heart and mind that your goal will be executed.

In the case of my Mary Kay career, I was determined and fixed. I had no problem telling people about my goals. Now trust me, the Incredible snatchers reared their ugly heads and told me that I was a fool to quit my "good job" to chase my dream. I had a "what is the worst that could happen mentality." Worse case, I could get another job but if I didn't step out on faith, I would never know if I had the power to live my dream.

Because the Incredible snatchers did not know anything about the God that I serve, they spoke against my dream with full power and conviction. But my conviction was stronger; it was greater. My God had already shown me His power and might so many other times and like I shared earlier, I knew too much about Him to ever consider doubting Him. So I continued on my quest to be the first and youngest black woman in my National Area to earn that prestigious "trophy on wheels." I was determined and more importantly, I was willing to do the work. As I have shared before, "faith without works is dead."

My faith lined up with my work and when they met, I had done it; I had executed my dream with enthusiastic expectation!

I may never forget picking up "Pinky the First." I sat in her plush seats and just let the feeling of a dream realized envelope me. It felt good; it smelled good. Man, that new car smell! I had arrived. I had broken a belief barrier for myself, family, community and unit of Mary Kay beauty consultants. Furthermore, it was done just five months after I walked away from my "good job."

I don't share this to brag on me, I share to brag on the abundance of the universe in which we live. God is no respecter of persons and if He did it for me, trust that He can do it for you as well. Although the reward was mine to turn heads as I drove around town; honestly, I cannot take all of the credit. First, credit is due and given to my Lord and Savior, Jesus Christ because He placed in me the ability to plan and strategize to make my dream a reality. Second, credit is due to the one hundred beauty consultants that were a part of the Dynamite Dream Achievers from April to September 2005. I have to admit that I did gloat a little. Now, I know that it wasn't right for me to do that but the thought of showing off my "I told you so," got me excited.

I had to let all of those Incredible snatchers know that I met along the way know that I could do anything to which I set my mind. I spent that first day in "Pinky the First" riding around strategically making drive bys to let them know that I had done what they said I couldn't do. I had seen the invisible and done the impossible and yes, you guessed it. My dream was Incredible.

It is exciting to know that I will forever hold that place in Mary Kay history for the state of Delaware and the Pam Tull National Area at the age of 28.

Anything is possible if you are willing to dream so big that only God can make it happen and while you are dreaming, you are willing to do the work necessary to make the dream a reality.

Incredible people ensure that they make a strategy and plan to execute their dreams and goals. They expect things to happen and are enthusiastic as they watch their strategies unfold. To become Incredible, you must consistently have a clear and thoughtful strategy. You must know what you need to do and when it must be done. You must commit now to writing it down so that you can stay on task and on purpose until completion has manifested itself. You must decide now that this strategy will help you avoid getting off track because that will not help you to close in on achieving the goal.

You must develop confidence. Goal setting and achieving is not for the faint at heart. You must make a non-negotiable decision now that it won't be over until it's complete. Even if the proverbial "fat lady" starts to sing, if you are not done executing your dream and goal, it cannot be over. You must be on purpose and target to ensure that your dreams happen.

So how will you execute your dreams and goals with enthusiastic expectation? By developing F.O.C.U.S. or following one course until you are successful. Oftentimes, we give up too early. If we would have just stuck it out a little longer, we would have realized that our strategy was viable and our goal would have been within our reach.

Additionally, I encourage you to develop a great support system of people who are where you want to be. If you want to be a speaker, get speakers to become your mentor. If you want to be an entrepreneur, you guessed it, make an appointment to talk with one and develop a relationship that will enhance your ability to execute your dreams. People who are where you want to be get excited about opportunities to help others get to their destination. Where applicable, be willing to pay for their insight if they will coach you as paying shows the value you believe they possess to help you achieve your goals. The Incredible You can't always expect a handout; don't get me wrong, sometimes, God will show you favor and you will get what you need for free but other times, it may be necessary to pay the piper.

The beauty about people who are Incredible is that they are not slighted by your dreams. Incredible people know that we do not serve a chump-change God and He can afford your dreams as well as theirs. As you become Incredible, remember principle two, and make sure that you have a heart ready to serve others so that when it is time to pay it forward you are primed and in position.

Lastly, I encourage you to take action by setting priorities. You cannot just sit still and expect your dream to become a reality. You have to do something. By establishing your plan of action, you will be able to set up

The Incredible You

your priorities and make it happen. As an example, it had been a dream of mine since high school to be an author. I even wrote a novel while I was in college with which I never did anything. For whatever reason, my dream was not real to me so it got stifled by the everyday things in life. But in 2007, I began to re-evaluate the dreams that I had for my life and I started to ask myself those all important questions: "Is there any reason why I couldn't give it a try?" "Why not me? Why not now?" The answer was a resounding "no," and "I can't think of a good reason." So I did it. I sat down to tell my story and finished my literary debut just a few short months later. Once the plan was set, I was ready to take action by setting up my priorities. I researched how to publish a book and today, I am a published author.

Whatever your dream or goal, it, too, is possible. Begin to plan and before you know it, you will be smiling at the reality of your heart's desire sitting in front of you on display as you loudly proclaim, "I did it; I am Incredible!"

Wisdom from my favorite book:
For he is strong that executes his word.

Unleash
Passion Abundance Confidence Expectation
Food for thought: Executing your dreams with the PACE Method.

Planning with Purposeful Passion:
What do you plan to do to show your enthusiasm about who you are? What does being enthusiastic mean to you? Is it a real thing or something that too much emphasis is placed on for you? Explain it in your journal.

Achieving with an Attitude of Abundance:
How important do you feel your attitude is when it comes to expectation? Have you read *The Secret*? Do you believe what the book says? Why or Why not?

Creating with Consistent Confidence:
What do you see being created in your life that will help you to enact this principle on a consistent basis?

Executing with Enthusiastic Expectation:
Of what you read in this section of the book, what resonated with you the most? What do you want out of life? What do you expect to get?

Principle Fourteen:

*Y*OU ALREADY POSSESS THE KEYS TO THE INCREDIBLE YOU.

Before you were born, God equipped you with every tool that you need to be Incredible. EVERY TOOL. So what stops you from acting like it? YOU. It's true the one person who stops you from experiencing the manifestation of your destiny spends time with you every day.

No amount of money, clothes, shoes, weight loss, hair, friends, loved ones and any other measurement you can think of will make any difference and/or influence the person that you will become. No matter how you try to slice it; your material possessions will never define the Incredible You. What does make a difference is You and the size of your mind. More importantly, your attitude and the positive and empowering places that you allow your mind to take you.

Once you expand your mind and consider the possibility that you can be Incredible without what the world defines as success, and simultaneously allow your mind to set you up for the success that has been ear marked as yours since the foundation of the earth, you will be able to walk it out. The Incredible You is about an expanded mind. Expansion will create exposure that brings everything that you desire into your life. Oliver Wendell Holmes was the first to say that a mind once expanded cannot return to its original though process because he knew the truth.

What does success mean to you? That is a simple enough question, right? Wrong. It may seem like it is easy enough to answer without much thought, right? When you look at this question this way, I am sure that your response would be based on the materialism of life. Your first thought was a big house, a nice car and a good job, right? It's okay, be honest with yourself, but my goal is that soon, your success will not be based on materialism; it will be based on those things inward, those things that no one can ever take away. Proverbs 16:3 says simply that "if you commit your plans to the Lord, they will succeed." That is awesome, right? So, according to the Word of God, simply developing a relationship with God and allowing His Word to resonate throughout your mind and spirit will lead you to success. Moreover, you already possess the keys to the Incredible You.

Living an Incredible life is much simpler than we all make it seem. An Incredible life is a mindset, a state of mind if you will. Very easily, you can take the lid off your thinking and move from forgettable to Incredible! Once you start living out on the branch where the fruit of life is, you will notice that everyday problems and obstacles no longer become hindrances or stumbling blocks that get in your way and keep you from fulfilling your Incredible life's dreams and goals. The steps to an Incredible life are simple:

First, consult God for everything you need, want, believe and dream. Make God your CEO. Give control over your destiny to Him, He will handle your dreams with care. He will line up relationships that are Incredible!

Second, evaluate and re-evaluate your associations – remember, you become like the people you spend your time with. As you go through this process, do not become dismayed. You will lose some people that you thought were friends. You will also gain some insight into the value that God has placed on the purpose that He birthed inside of you because those who walk away from you by choice or omission were blocking your view. Remember, people will never validate you; only God can do that. People won't get excited, empowered and motivated because He has already provided your validation! No matter what, do not hold yourself accountable for the ones who walk away; one monkey will never stop the show!

Each quarter, I make a list of the people who are in my space and I re-evaluate their place in my life. If, when I think of them, I am inspired and believe that they are an Incredible part of my world, they get a plus sign (+). If, when I think of them, I feel negativity or am perplexed at the thought of the value they add to my existence, they get a minus sign (-). You know the ones that when they call you say "Oh, I don't feel like talking to him/her. They always bring me down?" They get a big fat minus sign. If I feel absolutely nothing one way of another, they get a slash sign (/).

I am sure that by now you've guessed it, plus signs (+) get to stay! Minus signs (-) have to go and slash signs (/) have one more quarter to influence my life Incredibly so that they can stay or they have to hit the road. I do not have time for people who do not have my best interests at heart. I am going places that require positive sentiments and sincerity at all times and I cannot afford to let someone else that does not fit into my plan get to me in a manner that wastes my time. Time is the only thing I can never get back.

Constantly evaluating your associations will help to ensure that the Incredible person you are becoming does not get jaded or crowded by Incredible snatchers! As much as you love them, they've got very little place in your life.

Remember, your goal is to learn how to back away from the Incredible snatchers!

Next, make a Vision Board or Goal Poster. Habukkak 2:2 in the Old Testament of the King James Bible says "Write the vision and make it plain." It goes on to say, "Write it on tablets [goal poster or vision board]." Where are you going in this life? What does your life look like? Ask yourself the following question, "What can I begin to do today to make my life Incredible?" Follow that question with this one: "If I could be doing anything in the world and money was not an object, what would I be doing?" Then write it down. From there, brainstorm and come up with more ideas that all lead back to that first question.

An old business model says that "what gets attended to gets done"....You want to make sure that your 16x20 sized goal is back by a 16x20 sized POSTER or VISION BOARD. I mean, put everything on your vision board. If you are single and you desire to be married, find a picture of the ring you want to get when you get engaged. Additionally, list the qualities about your mate that will be important to you. What does your home look like? What kinds of children will you have? How many? Where will you vacation? The Bible says that we have not because we ask not. What that means to me is, I had better put it out there exactly how I expect to get it, and I encourage you to do the same. (That last statement is an example of executing with enthusiastic expectation!)

Just like when you go to the grocery store without a list you forget key items that you need at home, the same will be true of your goals. Write them down; write it down so that they can get attended to.

Don't believe that you will remember your dreams and goals, write them down. In fact, get some post-it notes and stick smaller versions of your goals all over the place to

The Incredible You

serve as a constant reminder that you can achieve anything to which you put your mind! Next, do something everyday that gets you closer to the vision you have for an Incredible life. Daily activity creates habits, habits create consistency, consistency creates confidence and consistent confidence is the gateway to dreams realized!

Lastly, live with Passion, Abundance, Confidence and Expectation. When you add P.A.C.E. to your life, life will begin. I want more than anything in the world to help you realize the importance of having P.A.C.E. When you learn how to plan with purposeful passion, you will find your reason for living. You will go from existing to living. Your heart will be warm and full when you start to achieve with an attitude of abundance. Attitude is truly everything and when yours is on point, everything else will fall into its rightful place. Confidence will change everything about who you are and who you want to be when you excel in creating it consistently. Lastly, expecting with enthusiasm will lead to execution skills that will be unparallel. I want God's best for you. I want you to be Incredible and enjoy every reward to which a P.A.C.E. lifestyle makes you entitled.

Remember, when you were born, God measured you with every ingredient you need to live your purpose in your Incredible life. All of the principles that have come before this one, I pray, help to solidify that God is doing His part. Before He formed you in your mother's womb, He already knew that if you did each of the following, you would be the Incredible creation that He predestined.

Trust that God has your best interests at heart. Have a heart that is ready to serve others. Experience life through eyes of faith. In all things, be grateful. An attitude of gratitude fills your cup. Never give up on yourself no matter what others may say. Create a life where everything is in proper balance and perspective. Release yourself from the issues, hurts and struggles of your past. Expect God's unmerited favor in your life. Decide that vision is your key to victory. Increase your self-image; you are who you say you are. Be Happy. Live to love. Execute your goals and dreams with enthusiastic expectation. Recognize that you already possess the keys to The Incredible You, believe it! Offer yourself the opportunity to overcome obstacles and adversity with passion and promise. Once you have done all of the above, you will be able to unleash God's promises for an Incredible life!

Wisdom from my favorite book:
Before I formed you in the womb I knew you; before you were born I approved you; I ordained you a prophet to the nations.

Unleash
Passion Abundance Confidence Expectation

Food for thought: Realizing you already possess the keys to the Incredible You with the PACE Method.

Planning with Purposeful Passion:
What is your plan to show that you have learned and embraced all of the principles that have come before this very important one? How is your passion level now?

Achieving with an Attitude of Abundance:
What have you already achieved from this book? Write it in your journal.

Creating with Consistent Confidence:
How is your confidence now? Have you created a plan of consistency to ensure that you continue to develop and explore it?

Executing with Enthusiastic Expectation:
Are your expectations being executed? Why or Why not?

Principle Fifteen:

OFFER YOURSELF THE OPPORTUNITY TO OVERCOME OBSTACLES AND ADVERSITY.

A setback is a set up for a comeback. The Incredible You will make mistakes. Let's face it. We all do and we will until we leave this earth. More importantly, there will be stumbling blocks that will sometimes get in the way. I can unequivocally promise you that without limiting my integrity in this and any future matters.

The way that you respond to life's challenges, trials and tribulations is what will make you Incredible. What will make a difference is your ability to look at the mistake and/or obstacle and learn valuable lessons that will prevent you from making the same mistakes again.

The only difference between a stumbling block and a stepping stone is how you choose to use it.

The Incredible You has to have a mindset that realizes that attitude is what makes all the difference. As previously discussed, attitude is 95% of the game. I hope that you can get excited that only 5% of your life is about skill! If you've got the right attitude, making mistakes won't rain on your parade in life, the mistakes will just cause a sprinkle. When it sprinkles, we don't even get wet, really. A few drops here or there never hurt anybody....right? Insanity has been described as doing the same thing yet expecting a different result. So, if you continually make the same poor decisions and come out of them unchanged, there is a problem and I must sadly confess that it is you.

Think about it this way, your obstacle and adversity can be construed as a crisis and, I would hate for you to waste it! What I mean is that the symbol for crisis was created by combining danger and prosperity together. Some of the most successful people in history have persevered and performed above expectation during a crisis.

It is time for the Incredible You to make a choice. Choose whether you want to be a coward and buck in fear at the thought of getting over it or, decide now to take a risk. What I know to be certain is that when you are in a crisis, it cannot get any worse so what's the worst that could happen? Think about it and then keep it moving. There is no sense in beating yourself up over what you could've, should've and would've done differently. It's over. Cut your losses and move on. Your best days are ahead of you and what is to come is better than what has been.

Give yourself permission to get over the obstacles. It is okay. You will arise from the challenge stronger, better, Incredible. If you don't feel that you have it in you, please seek help to get yourself on track. I saw a therapist for years and it helped me to let it go. There is nothing wrong with an objective third party who cannot and will not judge you helping you to sift through your past.

Can I keep it real with you?

Adversity and obstacles are a part of life. They will stop when you die. Until then, get use to them and when you are served lemons, grab the sugar and ice and make a glass of lemonade!

We've all had to overcome something. I was sexually abused as a child which led to increased promiscuity and unrealized self-worth that caused me years of headache and much more heartache; I also watched my mother get taken off to serve a jail sentence during my eighth birthday party. So what? It has made me stronger; it didn't kill me. I healed because I gave myself the opportunity to overcome the things that happened to me. I didn't blame my mother or even the sick man or cousins who sexually abused me. I decided to take the high road and P.R.E.S.S. on. I have decided to persistently run expecting supernatural success. I decided that God would be the Captain of my future and that I would allow the cycle of self-destruction to stop. I decided to replace the adversity with a positive outlook and the ability to dream.

Today, because I forced the obstacles to stop hindering my future, I am a talented empowerment speaker, author and entrepreneur who is able to mentor and coach men and women from all walks of life to live their dream.

Lance Armstrong, a world-class cycling star in his own right, learned that he had lung cancer and a 50% chance of survival in his twenties. Despite the news, he went on to win the Tour de France not once but four times. Oprah Winfrey also experienced forms of abuse and self-esteem concerns and her supervisors told her to change her name yet today; we all tune in to see "who's on Oprah." R.H. Macy made several failed business attempts before his department store Macy's became a staple in our retail society.

When people remember these Incredible people they don't talk about the obstacle, they discuss how they overcame! People are inspired and empowered by the stories of positive attitudes and the decisions made that show the world that we will not succumb to what the world has to say about us; instead we will make history! The four of us are positive examples that adversity, whether it comes about as the result of mistakes that we made in our own right, or just being in the wrong place at the wrong time, do not have to define the people that we will become.

A very important ingredient of becoming Incredible, is the ability to bounce back from adversity. Adversity is what qualifies you to be Incredible. The Incredible You will be defined by your ability to move forward and upward, toward achieving your mission in life, regardless of all the obstacles or other forms of adversity that are destined to come your way.

Consider the fact that you are most likely one of three kinds of people. Either you give up, you maintain or you reach. When you are the type of person who gives up, you will easily opt out, cop out, back out, and drop out. The minute you see something difficult coming your way, you give up and become convinced that you can't do anything right. When you give up, you use adversity as an excuse not to work hard. Sound familiar? If not, maybe you are a maintainer.

When you are a maintainer, you will be satisfied with never reaching your full potential. You will always go but only so far before you get comfortable and complacent; and complacency is devastating. You will never challenge yourself; you will avoid risk and, as a result, you won't progress in life. You will be an "if it's not broke don't fix it" kind of person. I'm sure that you agree that the Incredible you is not a maintainer!

Lastly, you may be a person who reaches for the moon and lands amongst the stars. When you are a person who strives, you will love learning, dreaming and executing all of your dreams with enthusiastic expectation. You will continually embrace and overcome challenges. You will see disappointments and obstacles as opportunities to keep it moving. You will make a non-negotiable decision to keep going no matter what obstacles life throws at you. You will be resilient and persistent. It may be challenging at times, but you have already decided that it will be worth it.

I know that I have already said this several times in this book, but I can't miss an opportunity to share it again: The only difference between a stepping stone and a stumbling block is how you use it. How will you use yours? To overcome, you must get comfortable in your own skin. Remember principle number ten, increase your self-image and be who you were created to be. Again, what God says about you doesn't change just because you or other people don't believe it. Push past the pain, forgive yourself and others who have wronged you and move on. The Incredible You is behind the adversity and obstacles. You are a survivor; you are Incredible.

Wisdom from my favorite book:
You, dear children, are from God and have overcome them, because the one who is in you is greater than the one who is in the world.

Unleash
Passion Abundance Confidence Expectation

Food for thought: Overcoming obstacles with the PACE Method.

Planning with Purposeful Passion:
Do you feel it is possible to live your passion without overcoming adversity? Why or Why not? If not, what are you prepared to do so that you can live your passion with purpose?

Achieving with an Attitude of Abundance:
Overcoming obstacles is a form of achievement. Describe how you have already achieved and what your attitude has meant to your journey. How will you identify the abundance in the issues of life that you have overcome? What can you change if you are still dealing with adversity that is preventing an abundant attitude?

Creating with Consistent Confidence:
What will confidence do to your ability to overcome life's adversity? Have the obstacles of life made you more confident? Why or Why not?

Executing with Enthusiastic Expectation:
What is your execution plan to enthusiastically overcoming your obstacles with an expectation that will prevent fear and doubt from hindering you? Expound on this in your journal today.

Principle Sixteen:

Unleash the Promises for an Incredible You.

The dictionary defines the word unleash this way: "set loose; to pursue or run at will." A second definition for unleash is "to abandon control of." I know that as a woman, being in control is pretty intoxicating. We love to know the who, what, when, where and why of everything that crosses our peripheral vision. I am not sure why, but we believe somehow that being in control of everything will order our lives better; but that is where we go wrong.

Abandoning control of certain aspects of your life, mainly your faith and ability to align your will with principle number one, or trusting that God has your best interests at heart, will ultimately lead to promises beyond belief in your life. When you set loose or pursue and run at will toward those goals, dreams and ideals in your life the experience will give you the passion, abundance, confidence and expectation that you desire. The Incredible You will emerge out of a cloud of doubt and walk toward an expectation of certainty that you can, will and must be Incredible.

You most assuredly have to position yourself to walk into the Incredible You. God's Word makes it clear what He has in store for you when you are obedient to His will. I love the Word of God because it allows you to put everything in proper perspective. To live an Incredible life, you have to prioritize your life so that God can work in

The Incredible You

you. As I see it, that proper order is God first, family second and everything else third. When you order your life this way, bountiful blessings will hunt you down and overtake you. Blessings and promises will be let loose upon you; they will be unleashed. Are you excited yet?

If you have taken the time to read this book and learn lots of useful information yet you fail to put it to use, or unleash it, then you just wasted a lot of your time! The New Living Translation of Job 36:11 says "if they listen and serve God, then they will be blessed with prosperity throughout their lives." I want more than anything for God's favor to overtake you. We have been through fifteen principles, the keys to the Incredible You as I see it and all of that will be in vain if you choose not to embrace the plan that the Creator has for your life.

God wants to do "exceedingly and abundantly above all we could ever ask of or think," according to Ephesians 6:20, but do you think that He will go against your free will? I hope that you are shaking your head "no," because you are correct; He will never go against your free will. If you want to get a hold of your promise, you must unleash the power to change your life, and it starts in your mind.

Malachi 3 discusses how when we commit to giving God a tithe (a tenth of our earnings, time, etc,) He promises to "open up the windows of Heaven to pour out blessings that we do not have room enough to receive." In other words, God promises to unleash, or set loose blessings upon our lives. So, I have a question for you....do you have room left? If so, then you need to rescind your control so that God can have His way in your life. He promised to overflow and overtake you with blessings...His Word is His bond and He will not tell you a lie. Trust me when I tell you that your spirit will thrive when you let Him have his way.

You must believe His Word and walk into His promise for you.

Every principle that we have covered in this book leads to this crescendo. If you don't make the right move at this time, all of your prior commitments and journaling, all of it will be for naught.

Every portrait is a work of art based on how the artist sees life and lived, it is my desire that you would make yours a masterpiece by aligning your life with the principles that I have shared. Want to make your life an Incredible masterpiece? You must be willing to unleash. If you want something you've never had, you must be willing to do something you've never done.

Remember GI Joe, the real American Hero? At the end of every show, he said "Knowing is half the battle." That statement is very true. Knowing *is* half of the battle. What you do with that knowledge is what produces the other half of the battle - RESULTS or Defeat!!!!

Do you know that you are not where you want to be? When you look back over your life, are you excited to see that you are living your destiny? Do you know that if you keep doing what you're doing you will get more of what you've got? Do you know that change can be simple? Do you know that life and death really do lie in the power of your tongue? Do you know that by speaking positive, living thoughts you can create change that manifests itself into your DESTINY?

ARE YOU READY TO WIN THE WHOLE BATTLE??? You must decide now to unleash God's promises in your life. All you need to do is make a decision; a non-negotiable decision that you are going some place different with your life. By deciding to take action and take the limits off your mind, you will unleash power upon your life. Remember, knowing is half the battle. With a made up mind, you can begin to propel yourself full throttle into your destiny. Taking massive action produces INCREDIBLE change - the kind of change that writes your own ticket to anywhere you want to go! Are you excited?

Expansion creates Exposure....

Do you realize that the average person has 60,000 thoughts a day? Sadly, most of the time, the thoughts the average person has are negative thoughts. Even though you don't actually speak them, through your internal language you are making it clear that you do not believe that you possess the keys and are ready, willing or able to unleash them in your life. I invite you to embrace today so that you can enjoy an Incredible tomorrow. Align your faith with your belief and know that what you believe will manifest in your life whether you are intentional about it or not. It is important that you take inventory of the seeds that your mind, mouth and heart plant each day and find the weeds so that they do not kill the fruit of your life. If you truly want to reap a harvest, you must ask yourself what seeds you must plant to get the fruit you want in your life.

The time is now to take the knowledge that you developed throughout this book and achieve results that will lead to developing into the INCREDIBLE YOU!

I think of unleashing God's promises much like I think about that awaited rain in the summer when we've been experiencing a drought – plants have died, grass is brown – bottom line everything is dying, including our spirits if we have not found a way to unleash the power of God's promises in our life.

The rain is such a simple thing. Do you ever take the time to just watch the rain? Each drop lands in a different spot. The exact spot where the drops fall was predetermined by God to ensure that the water gets to the exact area of your life that needs to be revived and refreshed; isn't that Incredible?!

God, the author and finisher of your faith, strategically places each drop from behind the clouds allowing there to be a mass production of living water in your life. Isn't that Incredible?

The rain allows the water to flow creating waves in our lives. Each wave has the ability to produce a reaction that can take us from normal to Incredible....will you allow the waves to come in and evoke the necessary change in your life? When the rain is over, we are left different. If we look closely, we should see tiny rays of color where the drops designed by God once fell. Those raindrops created rainbows, signifying God's promises in our lives. Now it's time for you to unleash those rainbows and walk full force into God's promises for you!

Here are some of the promises waiting to be unleashed in your life: a right to a life more abundant; unconditional insurance coverage; a bridge over troubled waters; your enemies will become your foot stool; and, if you in all your ways acknowledge Him, He will give you the desires of your heart.... now that's Incredible!!!

Wisdom from my favorite book:
And all these blessings shall come upon you, and overtake you, if you hearken to the voice of the Lord your God.

Unleash
Passion Abundance Confidence Expectation
Food for thought: Unleashing God's promises with the PACE Method.

Planning with Purposeful Passion:
How do you plan to unleash the promises and the principles discussed in this book in your life? What have you learned about your purpose? Is your passion alive and thriving? How so?

Achieving with an Attitude of Abundance:
What is your attitude now that you have finished the sixteenth and final principle of the Incredible You? Write about your attitude in your journal.

Creating with Consistent Confidence:
What are some of the things that you have created in your life as a result of this book? What is your confidence level? Has your definition of consistency changed?

Executing with Enthusiastic Expectation:
We talked about your plan to unleash God's promises in your life, how will you execute it? What do you expect to happen? Has your enthusiasm increased? Why is that important?

Seven Tips to Unleash The Incredible You

1. Get up two hours early each day. By doing so, you an order your day as such:
   - 5 minutes in gratitude
   - 15 minutes enacting the power of intention
   - 10 minutes reciting affirmations
   - 15-30 minutes reading something inspirational or empowerment in nature
2. Write and rewrite your goals each day in positive, present tense.
3. Plan your day in advance
4. Set priorities to each day, so that you can enjoy a daily win.
5. Use your car as a mobile university and listen to empowerment audios while you drive
6. Ask yourself two (2) questions after every experience you have:
   a. What did I do well?
   b. What can I do differently next time
7. Treat everyone as if they have a sign on their forehead which says "Make me feel Incredible."

About the Author

Darnyelle A. Jervey:
Author, Speaker, Coach & Consultant

A sought after speaker, certified life and business coach, award winning author and marketing consultant, **Darnyelle A. Jervey** is the founder of Incredible One Enterprises, LLC a full service small business development and empowerment firm that specializes in helping women to define and unleash the Incredible Factor for life and business success through keynotes, coaching, seminars and workshops. Her company introduces women in business to a unique formula for earning 6 figures in record time – mindset, marketing and money-making strategy. Darnyelle is known for her enthusiasm, contagious energy and passionate delivery as she builds dreams and potential in the lives of her audiences and workshop participants.

For **more than a decade**, Ms. Jervey has been capturing attention and keeping it as soon as she opens her mouth. Through intentional success in Corporate America where in three years she successfully progressed from a representative to a Vice President to her recent success as a **Top Pink Cadillac Executive Sales Director in Mary Kay Cosmetics**, Ms. Jervey has mastered the power of motivation and empowerment and successfully imparts that knowledge to everyone with whom she comes into contact.

In 2007, the manifestation of her purpose led to the development of Incredible One Enterprises, LLC. She is the producer of "**Own Your Incredible Factor**" a themed small business development and empowerment conference for women and the creator of other Incredible One Enterprises, LLC brands **Incredible Factor Coaching, Passionista Power Networking Events, The Incredible One Success Circle, An Incredible Moment with Darnyelle** and **The Incredible Factor Mastermind Program**.

Darnyelle A. Jervey

As a **speaker**, Jervey boldly shares her story...she's not supposed to be here...from health complications as a child and an incarcerated parent at an early age, she has consistently defied the odds proudly declaring herself a BBB - Belief Barrier Breaker. Jervey has shared the stage with Willie Jolley, Delatorro McNeal, II, Les Brown, Ephren Taylor, John Leslie Brown, Karen Taylor-Bass and Norma T. Hollis. Her speaking and coaching credits span conferences to women's ministries to College and University campuses. As an emerging powerhouse in the motivational speaking arena, Ms. Jervey is the author of 5 empowerment books: *If You Understood My Past, You Would Understand My Praise, The Incredible You, Dream the Incredible the Journal, Speak The Incredible and Maximizing the Incredible You.* Her next release is *Burn the Box: 50 Ways to Eliminate Obstacles, Facilitate Change and Overcome Adversity in Life & Business.* She is also currently writing her life's work, Unleash Your Incredible Factor.

Jervey has received the Black Achiever in Business and Industry Award as well as the Community Commitment Award in her home state of Delaware. She has been featured in Black Enterprise, Essence and Delaware Today magazines. She has appeared on various local and national television and radio shows. She is a member of the National Speakers Association, National Association of Women Business Owners, Speaker Match, Speakers of Excellence, Black Speakers & Experts, New Castle County Chamber of Commerce, Toast Masters, Intl, Delaware Black Professional Women, and the Middletown Area Chamber of Commerce. She holds Bachelors of Art degree in English from the University of Delaware and a dual Masters in Business Administration from Goldey-Beacom College.

To impact change in the lives of your group or organization, consider Ms. Jervey. She is destined to make your next event an Incredible One.

The Incredible You

Incredible One Enterprises, LLC
560 Peoples Plaza #255
Newark, DE 19702
www.incredibleoneenterprises.com
www.darnyellecoaches.net
www.darnyelle.com
888.801.5794

SPEAKING ENGAGEMENTS

Darnyelle has delivered over 500 motivational presentations at conferences and meetings nationwide and is available to speak at your next event.
Speaking Topics Include:
- Empowerment/Motivation/Inspiration
- Marketing/Branding/Sales/Closing the Sale
- Purpose & Passion/ Passionista Power®
- Team Building/Success / Attitude of Abundance
- Breaking Belief Barriers
- Being a Change Agent / Burn the Box®
- Confidence & Self-Esteem
- Overcoming Obstacles

For more information, a full catalog of all programs in the Incredible Factor™ Professional Development Series or the Incredible One Success Series™, to request a speaking packet or check speaking availability, please feel free to contact 888.801.5794 or info@incredibleoneenterprises.com.

You may also visit www.darnyellejervey.com www.darnyellecoaches.net www.incredibleoneenterprises.com or www.darnyelle.com.